THE COMPLETE SERAPHIN MESSAGES

TELEPATHIC COMMUNICATION
WITH AN ANGEL

Volume 8

Seraphin Messages 535 - 572
Received between July 2023 and September 2024

YOUR JOURNEY FROM CHAOS TO PARADISE

Rosie Jackson

**THIS BOOK IS DEDICATED
TO ALL READERS
AND ALL THOSE WHO SEEK ANSWERS**

May you be blessed with

intense curiosity,
deep compassion,
the desire to overcome all obstacles,
and the thirst to fully understand

for these will move you forward on your spiritual path,
enabling you to contribute to the
rebuilding of a new world

My deepest gratitude goes to Seraphin
for his trust and for the wisdom he has provided

Thank you to all translators, proof-readers and video makers
for their dedication to the Seraphin material

Rosie Jackson

Bibliografische Information der Deutschen Nationalbibliothek:
Die Deutsche Nationalbibliothek verzeichnet diese Publikation in der
Deutschen Nationalbibliografie; detaillierte bibliografische Daten sind
im Internet über http://dnb.dnb.de abrufbar.

Verlag: BoD · Books on Demand GmbH, In de Tarpen 42,
22848 Norderstedt
Druck: Libri Plureos GmbH, Friedensallee 273, 22763 Hamburg

Erste Auflage Oktober 2024

ISBN: 978-3-7693-0308-7

TABLE OF CONTENTS

Page

INTRODUCTION

Introduction to Volume 8 of
THE COMPLETE SERAPHIN MESSAGES

Dear Readers:

Every time I proofread the most recent batch of Seraphin Messages for publication in a new book, I note a rising feeling of excitement, lifting the vibration of every cell, paralleled by immense trust and calm. It would be true to say that the more I read in one "fell swoop", the more I fall in love with the messages, which – despite the passage of time - reveal themselves to be even more meaningful than when I first received them.

What is it that enthrals me?

The exquisite pearls of wisdom, the direct "no nonsense" manner of stating information, the wide-reaching cosmic perspectives, and above all, the undisputable knowledge that ALL WILL END WELL and that ALL IS IN DIVINE HANDS.

Yet Seraphin's teaching style has been under some scrutiny, so let me explain:

Seraphin's Teaching Style: Presenting Information

One criticism sometimes made of Seraphin's style is the lack of detail about events to come. To expose concrete plans would in-evitably lead to disappointment, due to the fluidity of celestial plans, influenced as they are by belligerent actions on earth and by the pace – or lack of pace - of human spiritual development. The physical and emotional state of Earth is also a fluctuating component. In some cases, it would also be dangerous to be privy to all details.

Another reason concerns the individual journey of each human being who will necessarily experience coming events in a very different way, again each according to their spiritual maturity, and according to where they are in different parts of the world. It is not possible to provide a description which will represent "reality" for each person on earth simultaneously. This is why Seraphin leaves "question marks" and avoids complete descriptions of future scenarios.

Seraphin's Teaching Style: Strict Approach

The strict tone which Seraphin mostly uses can be off-putting for some. Here I would say that the dire nature of our planetary circumstances merits very strong language demanding radical measures and solutions:

You may consider us very strict, but when you CLEARLY SEE your terrible misdemeanours and deviations from the "moral road", you will realise why a very firm hand – a celestial hand we might add – will be necessary to rule your world.

Seraphin additionally states:

Our tone today is necessarily extremely strict, for as we have been warning again and again, the situation is escalating and is arriving at its most acute "peak". And from then on, it is a roller-coaster feeling of plummeting to depths you never knew existed, at a speed you have never before experienced, involving emotional turmoil of a sort you thought you would never go through.

Seraphin demands the same clarity and integrity from us:

Fear and shock serve to paralyse and divide. Polarisation will occur, resulting in fierce arguments about which side "deserves to win" or which side is "better". But one simple fact is overlooked:

all conflicts have two aggressors. While there may be "justifiable reasons" for action, there is no point in determining which military is more justified to kill. There are no degrees of dead, just as there are no degrees of peace. You cannot have a "little bit of peace", just as you cannot have a "little bit of clarity".

The early Seraphin messages are more personal, gentle, poetic and meandering. However, the acute nature of the present situation when the whole fate of humankind appears to be hanging in the balance, requires determined and immediate action. Seraphin never hesitates to "get to the point" and he insists that it is no longer possible to avoid making important decisions or "sit on the fence". While he may sometimes sound daunting, he does so OUT OF LOVE, to awaken us before we are even more rudely awakened by shocking revelations and overwhelming events.

Seraphin's Teaching Style: Questions

Another hallmark of Seraphin's teaching method is asking questions in order to stimulate our self-reflection processes. Here are some examples from this volume:

When you are pressed against a wall, do you return hurriedly to the old circle or do you seek a new one?

Do you vacillate between the extremes of
I WILL EMANCIPATE MYSELF FULLY followed by
THERE IS NOTHING I CAN DO?

Do you clean your mental windows?

Do you close your mental shutters when the light is too bright, or when the truth is too much to bear?

Do you close your mind to unpleasant facts?

Can you bring back life to dormant desires?

Can you recognise decay?

*Where have you left your footprint,
and did it have a positive effect?*

If your life were a painting, what would it look like?

Do you see the unseen as well as the seen?

Do you see what is hidden as well as what is disclosed?

*Are you aware that your limitations, as you perceive them,
can always be broken?*

*Are you moving forward or do you automatically
retreat in self-protection?*

*Is it not time, Beloveds, to disperse with the superficial
and seek the SACRED?*

Let us now move on to the main topics
discussed in the messages:

Warnings, Prophecies and the Future

Encouragement, Empowerment and Potential

Awareness of Power, Responsibility and Mission

The Cosmic Perspective and Universe Management

Judgement Day

The Divine Plan

The Healing of Earth

Warnings, Prophecies and the Future

Readers sometimes tell me that it is debilitating to receive so many dire warnings. Sometimes this dampens their spirits to such a degree that they discontinue reading. I can only say that I personally find the warnings very necessary, since it is Seraphin's motivation to lessen the shock of sudden serious developments which might leave people paralysed if they have no prior knowledge. In essence, Seraphin wants us to have an "easy flight":

WILL YOU TRY YOUR WINGS
AND REGAIN YOUR ABILITY TO FLY?
IF SO, THE WINDS OF CHANGE WILL CARRY YOU,
AND YOUR FLIGHT WILL BE COMPARATIVELY EASY

The other "complaint" about prophecies is that they sound imminent, but they seem to take a long time to manifest, so some people lose hope and turn away. To this I would say that "closing down" a very complex and widespread global experiment, which is what this phase on earth has been, is necessarily a long process involving myriad interconnections, all dependent on each other.

Thus a few decades of preparation for closure is actually short compared with the thousands of years during which followers of Lucifer rebelled against celestial universe management. This rebellion was the catalyst for putting earth in quarantine initially. This period will end with the sudden eradication of "ungodly" trends on the planet, seeing the return of universe administration and strict adherence to cosmic law.

Seraphin warns that the moment WILL eventually come and that quick action is then required:

Be ready to "move" at any moment,
whether this means in actual fact,
fleeing a dangerous situation,
or whether it means "moving" away from your
beloved convictions and concepts.
Everything is destined to break,
apart from that which is DIVINE.
And in the end, only the DIVINE will remain.

What about the prophecies made by Seraphin?

Many references have been made to "great changes" beyond our comprehension, during which we will have to "let go" of much which is familiar, because it no longer serves humanity. This involves letting go of the nature of our relationships, of the constructs of our religions, and of all institutions and organisations which operate under false pretences. Seraphin states:

Whole new structures, experiences and parameters based on
DIVINE VALUES will appear overnight.
It is up to you to leave the "old" behind
and to march with determination towards the "new"

It is your mandate to
PROGRESS IN ACCORDANCE WITH DIVINE LAW,
and if you refuse to "move on",
and if you refute those laws,
then there is no hope for you.
We sound hard but we are actually
only furnishing you with facts.

Though many of Seraphin's statements may be seen as prophecies, he maintains that the coming phenomena and circumstances are in part a case of the cosmic law of balance kicking in:

The law which is always in effect
but which is manifesting results right now is
THE COSMIC LAW OF BALANCE.
Can you see how your world is out of balance?
Cosmic law stipulates that all imbalances
must eventually be redressed,
and that time is NOW.

Seraphin maintains that global inhabitants have failed to choose the Divine path, and so the balance must be redressed, and the shock will be more of an emotional one than anything else, because we will be shown the great extent of our discrepancies – the clash between firmly held beliefs and the *superstitious fragments of experience* they turn out to be. There will also be a very glaring difference between priorities upheld so far and the Divine mandate which we have collectively failed to follow.

Our gullibility will also be show-cased. The powerful short story entitled *The Roof*, included in this book, is an illustration of just how completely we have been manipulated, what prisons we have been living in, and what abundance exists beyond their parameters. Instead of "business as usual", we will be presented with the unadulterated truth:

It will be like trudging through a dark misty night, carrying an immeasurably heavy burden, without any hope of ever seeing the light of day, to the clouds suddenly parting and being blinded by the brightest light you have ever seen in your life.

Thus, the denouement of the complex and very negative circumstances on earth may seem long, and the fulfilment of the prophecies may appear to be delayed, yet Seraphin assures us that the final resolution will be sudden and will lead to an extremely bright future.

Encouragement, Empowerment and Potential

All Seraphin's warnings are balanced by his frequent attempts to encourage us, to empower us and to ensure us that we can get through this very difficult phase:

Your lives are guided with a view to
EXTENDING YOUR PERSPECTIVES, with regard to
INCREASING YOUR SPIRITUALITY, with regard to
INCREASING YOUR CAPACITY TO ASSIST OTHERS
and ultimately with regard to
INCREASING YOUR JOY

The light will come, thus heralding this step into new possibilities and certainly into new paradises which cannot compare with the mundane, numbed, humdrum lives which you stumble through today. We salute all those who are presently taking up the "spiritual sword" and who are forming part of the "spiritual army" as opposed to the military factions which presently still dominate your earth, but which are destined to fall.

Seraphin not only insists on our potential, he also insists on our divinity, if we choose it, and this hearkens back to the words of the Christ Jesus who said "You will do all this and more":

YOU ARE NOT RETIRING WALLFLOWERS
BUT CREATURES OF DIVINE POTENTIAL.
YOU ARE GOD,
AND INDEED ACTIVATION OF YOUR GODLINESS
IS THE ANSWER TO ALL ILLS.
The "missing information"
which could change the world for the better is that
YOU HAVE THE CAPACITY TO BECOME CHRISTS.
This means, in fact, that when you celebrate the Christ,
YOU SHOULD BE CELEBRATING
THE CHRIST IN YOURSELVES

Another comforting aspect is Seraphin's reiteration that the journey may be hard, but he assures us that it will bring new companionship, solidarity, joy and even "constant euphoria", if we live in accordance with cosmic law:

You will rejoice that you are now
in the company of travellers
OF THE SAME MIND,
WITH THE SAME GOALS,
SHARING THE SAME DISAPPOINTING HISTORY,
BUT ALSO SHARING THE STUPENDOUS GOALS
WHICH WILL PROPEL YOU INTO A
NEW ERA OF JOY, PROSPERITY AND PEACE –
A PEACE WHICH MEANS AN END TO ALL BATTLES

Will you plunge into this icy water, Beloveds,
knowing that it will turn into a warm and comforting bath?

The "warm bath" of which Seraphin speaks is the constant peace and joy from knowing that our choices are well made and lead to universal peace:

To see clearly is to be IN A CONSTANT STATE OF EUPHORIA,
because you can see all the results of any one choice, and you
are always in a position to make the right choice, if guided by
cosmic law which states that everything should be for the benefit
of humanity, and of course this benefits you as a member.

For those who cannot believe that they themselves are capable of "great things" and of having a positive effect, Seraphin often stresses the power of each individual, especially in combination with other individuals, as in his message ODE TO A DOT:

It is of the essence that you
CONTINUE TO MOVE FORWARD,
if only in baby steps,

*SO THAT MILLIONS OF BABY STEPS CAN
HAUL THE GREAT WAR MACHINE OUT OF THE MUD*

Seraphin reminds us often that together we have the ability to create peace and that this should be our common goal:

*If individuals are in charge of their emotions and practice integrity, diligence, dedication and sincere self-reflection daily, then the collective result is
INDESTRUCTIBLE PEACE.*

And in all this, Seraphin and other members of the spiritual hierarchy which govern outside of our planet pledge their support and let us know that they have our "backs":

*Know that we are ever progressing towards our mutual goal, which is the denouement of all which is evil,
to be fully laid out in front of your very eyes,
to the winding down of this planetary phase on your earth, leading to future renewal.
In this, many of you will play a major role.*

Awareness of Power, Responsibility and Mission

Seraphin knows that everyone reading these messages at this time has an important mission to pursue, even if this sounds like a stupendous and impossible statement. Many may feel clueless, but knowing that we have collectively produced our present negative situation goes hand in hand with knowing that we can change our behaviour and have a positive outcome. While living in complete awareness of all choices is a very demanding way to live, it results in taking ultimate responsibility for our own lives and improving them:

You are also on a mission which breaks
ALL THE BOUNDARIES OF YOUR
PRESENT COMPREHENSION and which – once you set of
with dedication, determination and trust in that direction -
IS MORE THAN POSSIBLE.

You will soon learn that you and many other inhabitants on this
planet have taken an ENORMOUS DETOUR from your original
mission. The proof of this is that your mission is largely not clear
to you, and you have not actively searched for that what is truth,
or for that which elates you, or for that which simultaneously
gives your life and the lives of others more meaning and quality.

Seraphin's guidelines and goals for us, described in a general
way, are as follows:

ATTEMPTING TO REACH THESE HEIGHTS OF PURITY,
PERFECT INTEGRITY, MEASURED REACTIONS
AND ABSOLUTE SERENITY IS YOUR GOAL.
AND IT IS YOUR GOAL ALSO TO SERVE AS
A TEMPLATE FOR OTHERS TO FOLLOW

Seraphin reminds us that everything we think, everything we
learn and every step we take is a *PIONEERING EXERCISE*
FROM WHICH THE REST OF HUMANITY MAY PROFIT.
Please see also the important message entitled YOUR LIFE IS
AN ARTWORK, which likens living to the creative process which
exerts influence on the viewers:

You may proceed at your own pace, you may choose your own
colours, you may choose what to portray, and you may choose
whether or not it may benefit the spectator. Know that spectators
there always are, even if you live apart as a hermit in a distant
realm. Your task is to manifest the DIVINE in your artwork, in
whatever fashion you choose, and thus can it serve as an inspi-
ration to others who are not so far along the path.

Another very important message in this collection is called *THE DIRE CONSEQUENCES OF DENIAL OF IMPACT AND DENIAL OF CONTACT*. If we deny that our actions have consequences, and that they do not impact anyone else, then we are free to do as we please without regard for others. This is one of the main creeds of the Luciferian Rebellion – that altruistic motives are misplaced and irrelevant, and that one can flourish perfectly well when one is independent of the DIVINE WHOLE.

Because the Luciferians abdicated responsibility, except for themselves, Seraphin never hesitates to remind us of our responsibilities, even in the darkest of times. Here is a selection of some of his more stringent statements from this collection:

IT IS UP TO EACH ONE OF YOU TO DETERMINE
WHICH WAY THE SCALES WILL TIP.
YOU ARE NOT RETIRING WALLFLOWERS
BUT CREATURES OF DIVINE POTENTIAL.
Ideally, you will USE THE DARKNESS to experiment with
everything which produces "light" and which raises the vibration.

IT IS YOUR DUTY ALSO to point out
THAT WHICH IS NOT SACRED,
FOR IT HAMPERS EVERYONE ON THE PATH DIVINE.

It will not be possible to ignore the increasing "icy winds"
or the consequences thereof.
It will not be possible to ignore the damage and cries for help.
Nor will it be possible to ignore any more
ALL THAT WHICH IS VALUABLE WHICH HAS DIED.
The moment you "awake" to this,
the moment your mind is involved in this process,
the more you are
BLAZE TRAILING A LINE OF THOUGHT
FOR OTHERS TO FOLLOW.

You should be aiming for ABSOLUTELY PURITY OF MIND,
which will inevitably lead to behaviour motivated by
good intentions and by compassion
and which also immediately pinpoints
ALL THAT WHICH IS NOT SACRED,
singling it out for immediate extermination.

Thus, Seraphin emphasizes our responsibility both to act as a role model and to exercise strict critical awareness, locating and eradicating forms of behaviour which are obviously at odds with our sacred role.

The Cosmic Perspective and Universe Management

One of the most difficult new concepts which Earth's inhabitants will have to wrap their minds around is the "extra-terrestrial presence" both on and off the planet which has existed for time immemorial, but which has been deliberately hidden from public view. Our "prison world" status has much to do with this, blocked off from our cosmic brethren who we might otherwise harm or contaminate. To sum this up extremely briefly: despite all the violence, insanity and abuse on our world (which has been "allowed" for purposes of exposure, spiritual development and recognition of crimes), the celestial hierarchy always holds the reins;

The members of the universe administration have seen so much, have had so much experience and have been so active on many unseen levels that it is impossible to make a faulty move. It is as if ageless beings of ultimate serenity and wisdom are at the helm, which is indeed the case. Are you ready for this? We suspect not, for it has not been your training to expect "galactic outsiders" to enter into your reality, but we say to you that this is inevitable.

EARTH IS SUBJECT TO UNIVERSE GOVERNMENT,
WHICH RULES IN ORDER TO SERVE ALL CITIZENS
SO THAT THEY CAN REALISE THEIR BEST ENDEAVOURS
IN SERVICE TO THE ONE.

Seraphin frequently stresses the importance of the law of one, which he explains in following way, and this is where it gets really "mind blowing", for he maintains that one thought from us can *"CAUSE UNIVERSES TO PLUNGE INTO DARKNESS OR TO SAIL INTO THE LIGHT".*

You are not only connected to your neighbour BUT TO EVERY-ONE ON EARTH, in the sense that everyone is your neighbour, and you are all affecting each other for the better or worse, depending on your choices. BUT WE SAY TO YOU THAT THE CONSEQUENCES ARE HUGE, BEYOND YOUR IMAGINA-TION, AND BEYOND YOUR PLANET BECAUSE THE REST OF THE UNIVERSE IS POPULATED WITH YOUR NEIGHBOURS.

This is one of the greatest challenges you will be faced with, because it involves

MINDFULNESS OF EVERY STEP AND EVERY INTENTION OF YOUR JOURNEY, IN THE FULL KNOWLEDGE THAT AS YOU MOVE, TRILLIONS OF BEINGS AND PLANETS MOVE WITH YOU, AND KNOWING THAT ONE POSITIVE OR NEGATIVE THOUGHT WHICH YOU SEND OUT INTO THE COLLECTIVE CONSCIOUSNESS CAN TIP THE BALANCE, CAN MAKE THE DIFFERENCE, CAN CAUSE UNIVERSES TO PLUNGE INTO DARKNESS OR TO SAIL INTO THE LIGHT.

And to end this section on the cosmic connection, here is Seraphin's description of how everyone is connected to the central universe:

The central universe, like a distant, multi-coloured, magnificent disc or star, huge and multi-facetted and of the highest possible "love vibration", is connected to you as if by a thin thread travelling through space. This is tied to your inner divine core.

Judgement Day

The Day of Judgement has been prophesied in various religious texts, but perhaps it would be more appropriate to call this "assessment day", adjudicated by the "celestial judges" which Seraphin mentions below. It involves a long hard look at how we have spent our lives and whether it can be considered a worthy body of positive learning experience. Seraphin tells us that this cannot be avoided and that THE DIVINE is the yardstick against which we will be measured:

Know that all these paintings of your lives, which reflect all your choices and creations during life, are going to be put on show in an enormous art gallery. They will be seen and reviewed by celestial judges. They will be assessed for their meaning, beauty, beneficial effect and legacy. They will be sorted into those which inspire and those which depress. They will be scrutinized for potential, for signs of openness to change, for proof of a benevolent attitude towards others.

In the end (AND THAT DRAWS NEAR!) no deviations from the DIVINE will be tolerated. It is best to take NOTHING with you so that you can progress at ease. To pack large and cumbersome suitcases full of possessions, convictions and memories is to drag yourself down.

In view of all this, it is perhaps easier to understand Seraphin's sense of urgency and his "no nonsense" delivery of recommendations to humankind.

The Divine Plan

What is the Divine plan of which Seraphin often speaks?
The important message GARDEN OF SOULS
provides a clear answer:

*IT IS A MAJOR STRATEGY ON MYRIAD LEVELS TO
CLEANSE YOUR EARTH OF
ALL NEGATIVE FREQUENCIES,
CONFLICTS AND CONTAMINATION,
AND TO REPLACE THOSE WITH HIGH FREQUENCY
MATERIALS, EVENTS AND INTENTIONS WHICH WILL
LEAD TO COMPLETE PEACE AND PROSPERITY
ON EARTH FOR THE WHOLE OF HUMANITY*

*Earth, therefore, is a special garden where seeds – in effect
YOURSELVES – are provided with the opportunity to grow, not
only physically as a result of the gifts which nature generously
presents to you, but also SOUL GROWTH in the form of various
experiences and learning lessons which are ONLY TO BE
FOUND HERE. And you have taken the decision to take all this
on, even before incarnating, and after long discussion with various guides whose aim will always be YOUR SOUL GROWTH.*

*Many of you here have deliberately chosen one of the
STEEPEST LEARNING CURVES THAT HAS EVER BEEN.*

According to Seraphin, the Divine plan involves the complete
termination of evil, although evil is first allowed to run its course,
giving the perpetrators "enough rope to hang themselves" in full
view of everyone. Here are a number of relevant references:

*In one way, the "ungodly" is allowed to play out, rather than being
nipped in the bud, SO THAT IT CAN BECOME VISIBLE TO ALL.
It is only following this visibility that it will be fully understood by*

all. Then it will be clear that godly countermeasures are fully jus-tified and fully necessary. This is what we mean by the necessity to take a step back, allowing tragedies to unfold, allowing secrets to surface and allowing evil to raise its terrible head, in order to move forward AS ONE with full understanding of the fact that the termination of evil is completely necessary and THE ONLY WAY.

You can be sure that the celestial hierarchy has considered all options and that it will always choose an option which will "wake up" the most people, thus providing an opportunity to further spiritual maturity. The hierarchy will always choose an option which TAKES AS MANY SOULS WITH IT AS POSSIBLE.

You will be required to do one mental "U-turn" after another, in an extensive and exhausting learning program

This is such a huge topic that we inevitably fail to do it justice here in these few short sentences, yet know that the celestial hierarchy is keeping the "Earth garden" under close observation and will provide clear instructions so that all "seeds" on earth will have optimal conditions to grow. Those which do not manage to germinate now, on the other hand, will be removed to different "soil" and to conditions more suitable to their slower pace of spiritual growth.

The Healing of Earth

In future, the healing of our planet will be a huge focus and priority. Seraphin makes it very clear that our personal life choices either benefit or harm her.

In *Seraphin Message 554:*
TIED TO THE LAND: YOUR FATE AND FUTURE,
Seraphin delivers a message from our earth, Gaia:

It is our duty to carry this message from Gaia to yourselves.
It is a message of great love, for she sees and therefore
understands EVERYTHING which is going on
as you move and act on her skin.
Her ability to discern is acute.
Her knowledge of your habits and emotions is great,
for she feels them all as if they were her own.
AND THEY ARE, BECAUSE YOU ARE ALSO HER.

It is therefore with the deepest regret that she informs you
THAT SHE CANNOT CONTINUE IN THIS WAY.
SHE MUST TAKE ACTION TO
COUNTERACT THE ACCUMULATED NEGATIVITY.
IF SHE DOES NOT DO THIS,
IF SHE DOES NOT COME TO A COMPLETE STANDSTILL,
IT WILL BE THE END OF HER,
AND THUS IT WILL ALSO BE THE END OF YOU.

THIS WORLDWIDE PAUSE WILL FAST-TRACK
THE GERMINATION OF NEW IDEAS,
NEW PROJECTS AND NEW WAYS OF BEHAVIOUR,
ALL BASED ON NEW PRINCIPLES.

You will see her wounds, the blemishes on her skin, the areas of devastation, death and destruction. All this will you feel personally, and thus will you know that your personal choices either benefit or destroy her. You will be the GUARDIANS of every city, every river, and all physical spaces. When the Earth is a global healing room (and we assure you that this is an obligatory step after so much deviant behaviour and actions throughout millennia) every space must become surveyed, protected, and made holy. There will be no more ruins, dumps or wastelands of rubbish.

In the end,
EVERY ROOM IN EVERY BUILDING
WILL BECOME A HEALING ROOM.

And so, with this vision of our earth as one enormous "healing room", I come to the end of my introduction. My great thanks go to you, the attentive reader, who will be part of this transformation on earth. My unending gratitude goes to Seraphin for entrusting his words to me. Rosie Jackson, October 2024

Detail from THE HEALING ROOM by Rosie Jackson

Seraphin Message 535
THE CASE FOR NOTHING

Through Rosie, 9th August 2023

There is no way, Beloveds, that ANYONE is going to escape the future feeling of being completely overwhelmed and completely "out of their depth". You may recall, if you are somewhat older, severely difficult experiences such as the death of a parent or the stress of leaving something else you love behind.

When you receive such news, and when the reality of it truly "sinks in", it is as if time has stopped and you are often incapable of doing anything.

For many, crying is also something which does not come easily, although it is also part of the healing process. There are those who manage to pull themselves together but who do not truly manage anymore because they have not taken part fully enough in the grieving process.

So, what will you do, Beloveds,
when the world grinds to a halt?
Will you rail against the injustice of it with all your might?
Will you sink into fear and kill yourself?
(and yes, death through fear is possible).
Will you recognise this standstill as the result of the
STANDSTILL IN YOUR HEARTS?
Will you recognise that those who
STILL CANNOT LEARN AND WHO
STILL CANNOT SHOW COMPASSION
HAVE NO PLACE ON THIS EARTH?

You will lose many people, Beloveds. You may have suspected beforehand who would survive the sorting process, and who would not survive it. But believe me, your picture is incomplete and you can never actually know the destiny of any one soul, the saddest thing being that:

MOST PEOPLE ON EARTH HAVE NO INKLING
THAT THEY HAVE A TASK OR DESTINY, LET ALONE
MANIFEST THEIR VISIONS FOR OTHERS TO SEE.

Thus, you will inevitably be bereft of many familiar faces. Add to this, many familiar places, for the face of the earth will also change. Comfortable and known procedures, customary habits and customary ways of behaviour WILL ALL HAVE TO CHANGE SO THAT THIS DREADFUL SCENARIO WILL NEVER AGAIN ARISE.

You may ask: "What will remain?", and we will reply "the wind blowing through your hair, the sun shining on your face, and your positive mind-set". And yes, you have a positive mind-set – otherwise you would not have been able to progress so far.

You may ask: "What will be new?" and now we get to the exciting part: new knowledge, new technologies, new freedoms, new opportunities, new insights and new cosmic sisters and brothers.

The most important insight will be that you are unswervingly on a spiritual path, and that this path is NOTHING LIKE THE ONE YOU WERE FOLLOWING PREVIOUSLY. And this is where the title of this piece comes in: it is best to take NOTHING with you so that you can progress at ease. To pack large and cumbersome suitcases full of possessions, convictions and memories is to drag yourself down.

This may seem very radical to you, but this is an occasion where you will have to look at EVERY SMALL DETAIL and decide whether it serves the new divine plan or not. If you do so, you will conclude that VERY LITTLE is suitable for continuation. There is no room for compromise in this, for if every individual on earth makes compromises, the damage is done and you will again veer off on an insalubrious tangent towards global depravation.

Yes, global depravation is what you will see with your very own eyes, and you will not be able to believe the depths to which your fellow humans have sunk. You will also "sink into the ground" when you realise how you personally have allowed this to come to pass, if only in that you did NOT QUESTION ENOUGH.

New times are rolling on, Beloveds, and one day they will strike you hard with all their might. Be ready. Seraphin

Seraphin Message 536
CHOICES: THE DETERMINING FACTOR

Through Rosie, 19th August 2023

Inhabitants of earth! This is one of the most important questions which you will ever ask yourselves, and that is:

ARE YOU ALWAYS AWARE OF YOUR CHOICES?

With this, we do not necessarily mean the "life-changing" decisions which may immediately pop into your head when you read this question – the decision to move, the decision to select what sort of work you want to pursue, or the decision of who you choose as your partner - even if these major decisions and turning points have had a considerable impact on your life.

We are talking about the decisions and choices which are ongoing, for example when and how do you react to a certain word, or situation, or calamity, or joyful news. These decisions are indeed constant.

For many people on earth at the present time, these choices are far away from their thoughts. They are on "automatic" as far as many choices are concerned: they follow already familiar paths, they automatically follow any path suggested to them by others: they seemingly involuntarily pass through every day in the same way, feeding the same habits, meeting the same people in the same way, avoiding the same challenges and never questioning the same "irregularities".

To live in complete awareness of all choices is a very demanding way to live, yet it results in you taking ultimate responsibility for your own lives. You realise that what you "put in" to life, even in the smallest moment, will cumulate and form part of some later result which is presented tangibly before your eyes. It is the knowledge that – in every moment – the law of cause and effect is in play, and is playing out, even if the majority have no concept of this.

Your "good" and continuously "good" choices are essential to your health, your peace of mind, and ultimately essential for the peace and good health of the planet, who carries all the consequences of your positive and negative actions. Suffice to say that the negative actions surpass the positive ones and that she is "out of balance" as a result. And tipping too far in one direction inevitably means that one will fall over in the end. Your earth is very near that point.

How quickly do you choose to jump in and save someone who is drowning? How quickly do you rush for water if you see a fire? How quickly do you take someone in your arms when they are upset? Your reaction times are important, and your reaction times regarding earth's ailments is certainly less than slow.

You may say that you are only one person and that your actions will not "count" for much. But in this you are wildly mistaken.

Your energy always carries. Your positive thoughts will always benefit the receiver. Your "positive" actions will always return to you on a personal level.

The ultimate choice has not been granted to you, you may argue. And this is the choice of incarnating on this planet. However, know that this was also your choice, and that you choose the most excellent position and circumstances to experience exactly that which you wanted to experience. Perhaps you have the idea that you would only like to incarnate onto planets where everything is in harmony, where there is no work to do, and indeed no one to help, because everyone has a high standard of living and perfect health. Perhaps you have the idea that life should be a party and that this would be a great way to live.

We are not condoning suffering here, for we know that many suffer on your earth, but would it not be a glorious choice to go forth and determine to lighten the load of such humans who have not yet found their way and who have not yet succeeded in establishing such a society?

And so those who read this or who are on a similar spiritual path can be assured that their choice of coming to planet earth is indeed glorious, even though it may not seem like that for the most part. Experiencing hardship, like the majority is unfortunately necessary to understand hardship, and to sympathise with others for whom it is a daily experience.

To oneself succeed in dragging oneself out of adverse circumstances (no party at all!) is also a huge inspiration for those who have not yet succeeded to get themselves out of the mire.

This is why you are so valuable to earth's inhabitants: you share their experience, and therefore you have compassion for their plight, yet you also serve as a role model FOR THOSE WHO

WANT TO RESURFACE INTO FULL AWARENESS AND WHO
WANT TO FOLLOW A MORE GODLY PATH.

Do not underestimate the value of your journey here. The choices
– which are getting more acute by the minute – are increasing in
pace and intensity until there will only be one choice left: to go or
to stay. And this will be dependent on one's ability to learn and
change one's behaviour. We would like to remind you of all this
as we approach the final deadline by which this choice must be
made. Seraphin

Seraphin Message 537
THE GREAT FLOWERING TO COME

Through Rosie, 29th August 2023

You will become very depressed, inhabitants of Earth,
if you focus exclusively on the negative aspects of your world,
for example on the many millions who have died
and are still dying through wars and human trafficking.

Of course, there are some who go in completely the opposite
direction, waltzing naively through life, without a care, with their
heads in the clouds. One might suppose that they are supremely
and eternally happy, despite what happens around them, yet
without critical assessment of the present situation, they will also
descend into depression because they will (at some stage)
realise how "dislocated" from reality they really were.

Those who focus on purely negative aspects are labelled "pessi-
mists" or "conspiracy theorists" by those who float unperturbed
through life, building their own little worlds and rarely looking
beyond them.

Where are you on this scale of action versus passivity, in the face of depravity or on the scale of awareness? Do you recognise the consequences? Can you still feel joy? Can you hold the balance, or do you despair?

Do you reward yourself in abundance – or rather over-abundance – so that you can continue to "hold out" in the face of widespread corruption and destruction? If so, you are contributing to the decline, as your interest in implementing change is diminishing, while your debilitating addictions increase.

It may seem obvious to some of you, but this is not the time to vegetate. It is the time to sow seeds. The seeds will probably not have the right atmosphere or conditions to grow, because all-pervading circumstances are very unfavourable STILL. But the time will come when there is enough "rain" and "sun" for germination, and then it is essential that the seeds have been placed in readiness, for they will be SO NEEDED, and people will THIRST AFTER THEM BECAUSE THEY WILL PROVIDE HOPE AND PRESENT NEW WAYS OF ENCOURAGING GROWTH, COMPANIONSHIP, UNITY, AND THUS HAPPINESS.

Therefore; if no one is interested in your present offerings, of whatever kind - although you yourself are well aware of their intrinsic value, their potential to heal and their ability to offer new, positive perspectives - do not despair. Instead, continue with quiet confidence and determination in the certain knowledge THAT YOUR DAY WILL COME and that the seeds you have sown will inevitably result in THE GREAT FLOWERING.

Remember this, Beloveds, when your hearts are heavy, when you are dejected through lack of visible response, when you are faced with an empty room instead of an audience of interested faces, for the time will come when you will be sought after as never before, and then your efforts will no longer be directed towards trying to attract interest, but rather you will be fighting for a few free moments to yourself.

You will have new challenges – how to remain calm and balanced at all times, how to regenerate properly so that you can present your very best, and presenting your very best will be your constant aim.

And so we leave you with these thoughts, urging you as always to seek growth but also balance in every situation. Seraphin

Seraphin Message 538
HITS, HURRICANES AND HARVESTING

Through Rosie, 6th September 2023

In a moment of heaviness and lack of direction, this scribe just asked what to do next, and she was presented with the word PURPOSE.

We would like to ask you whether you are following your purpose, every second of the day. This does not mean, take no rests: it means DO NOT LET YOUR PURPOSE ESCAPE YOUR EYES.

You may argue that you have no purpose. If so, IT IS TIME TO SEARCH FOR IT. And we know it can be hard in these times of great confusion, great violence and – yet again – great lack of direction. Let purpose compass your path. Let this uplift you to the stars. Let this be a guarantee (which it actually is) that everything will improve and that you had a part in it.

Meanwhile, though, on this present earth plane, many of you are feeling tired and jaded, wondering if the "purpose" you have followed so far is indeed the right one. It is good to continually question: thus will you eventually reach perfection, improving on yourselves daily, and increasing the quality of the skills which benefit others on a constant upward moving scale of excellence.

But there is another factor involved: you are afflicted by tiredness, listlessness and lack of purpose, and this - COMBINED WITH THE GREAT FORCE OF INCOMING COSMIC ENERGIES, is making it more difficult to move in directions which are not in alignment.

What do we mean by this?

If you find it increasingly difficult to go in a desired direction, THIS IS BECAUSE YOU ARE BEING PREVENTED!
This means that you are invited to reflect upon whether another direction might not be more appropriate.

We have talked about this before. The incoming energies will take their toll on you if you fail to rise to their standards and "vibration". Physical tiredness or illness may be a result of such "hits". Hits may also crush you in the sense that they will force out all suppressed emotions. You may be laughing one minute and crying the next. This is all part of the cleansing process.

The cleansing process continues on a greater scale also. Not only you may be crying, but the earth also, resulting in hurricanes, floods and storms, and those of you who have been observing the "news" will note the increase in these worldwide.

What is all this "cleansing" leading to?

It is earth's method of sorting out what she wishes to keep. If you consider the harvesting of fruit, it is of course possible just to load it all onto big trucks, push it into huge vats and see what comes out at the other end. Consider though that if picked by hand with the utmost care, the mouldy parts will be removed, as well as insects or wasps, and this will result in food of excellent quality.

This is what the earth now requires – excellent quality, thus will the harvesting be methodical, painstaking and radical so that only the best remains. You can apply this metaphor to practically everything you see around you, BECAUSE EVERYTHING IS ON EARTH AND PART OF HER.

We wish you strength in the time to come. As we have said before, it is your choice whether you wish to rise to excellent standards, or to let yourself go. Seraphin

Seraphin Message 539
RISE, FALL AND CRASH

Through Rosie, 22nd September 2023

Regard the waves of the ocean, Beloved inhabitants of Earth at this present time (though many of you will not be remaining long term). Take some time to look at the ocean, in person if possible, not for a minute but for more than an hour. You will see the waves rise, fall and crash, in that order, in very regular patterns.

Do you think that ANYTHING IS GOING TO STOP THIS?

Similarly, do you think that ANYTHING is going to stop the larger cycles at work, all of which have an influence on your reality without your present knowing?

BUT KNOW THAT THERE IS A GREAT CRASH AHEAD. And like the falling of a great wave, nothing can stop this momentum.

You will feel the devastating side effects once it has crashed. The wave will bring a mixture of scorching naked truth, the absolute necessity to implement radical change immediately, and the challenge of having to move on, leaving everything behind.

You will cease to focus on your appearance, your status, your financial state, your next party and your next holiday (just to give you a few examples).

You will be physically stranded, moving in ever decreasing circles, and yet your mind – if open – has the potential of expanding in a huge manner, similar to a pebble landing in a pool.

The impact point may be small, but the ripples – i.e. the implications as regards the opportunities to grow – are enormous.

We ask you to go within and ask yourselves if your minds can remain open, and if you can leave all old mind-constructs and fixed ideas behind, while at the same time being confronted with severe physical limitations.

We cannot describe here exactly what will befall you, for firstly it will be a different mental and emotional experience for everyone, and secondly it would "pre-empt" or even prevent your learning experience to reveal it in advance.

Yet we are here to again give you advanced warning of a general nature.

Seraphin

Seraphin Message 540
ODE TO A DOT: ODE TO YOU

Through Rosie, 4th October 2023

To most of you, a dot will seem like an incredibly insignificant and small thing, to be put at the end of sentences or under question marks. Yet if used appropriately, it can have an enormous effect. We refer you to the paintings of this scribe where dots are used in all sorts of ways – in all sorts of positive ways, we may add. You would never imagine the changes which these dots have actually instigated because you are only presented with the finished effect. You are not presented with the very long painting and repainting process.

In the beginning, you might not notice that there are dots there at all. Yet if you look "under the covers", if you pursue investigation on a visual level, you can see more, and of course there are many parallels which we can draw here. Let us see what a dot can achieve, especially in combination with other colours, other surfaces and - above all - other dots.

A line of dots can emphasise contrast and assist clarity. It can increase the vitality of a duller background. It is often the dot which creates new areas by establishing spaces "in-between". It is the dot, with its round edges, which allows you to "peep through". It is the dot, when assembled with other dots, that increases intensity, provides depth, tempers excesses and elevates mediocrity, creating a completely different impression which carries a much higher vibration.

What is the effect of putting a black dot on a white surface? Suddenly it is the focus and the purity of the white surface has been sullied.

What is the effect of a white dot on a black surface?

Suddenly the dark has been penetrated.
Suddenly there is a focus on light.

What is the effect of putting a white dot on a white surface? It cannot be seen, but it is still there.

What is the effect of putting a black dot on a black surface? It cannot be seen, but it is still there, contributing to the darkness.

Even though unseen, nothing is lost in the universe.

One dot may stand alone. Two dots have the potential of becoming the beginning of a chain. A chain connects dots and strengthens joint (and here we would say godly) purpose. It is three dots together which form a triangular group with maximum stability, a reflection of the TRINITY.

A line or a chain of dots can always be extended, and in an evenly spaced line, each individual dot can be clearly seen. Yet if dots are painted directly on top of each other, only the dot on the very top can be seen at all. The shade of colour of the dots in a pile may intensify, yet the power of individual dots is undermined. Examine in this regard your social and organisational structures.

A curved line of dots can turn into a circle. A straight line of dots will always have a leader, and a renegade. They may cross other lines of dots at various stages, but the individual dots never change their position, and they are never united as one.

A dot can look like a dot, or it can look like a hole. It is all a matter of perspective. Dots can make sharp edges more gentle, and they can give gentle edges more definition.

What does the perfect painted dot need? It needs a steady hand, compassed by the wisdom of knowing where it should be perfectly placed, holding a perfectly poised paintbrush, holding a drop of paint with the perfect turgidity.

If there is too much water, the dot becomes transparent.

If it is too thick, the dot cannot be placed evenly on the canvas, causing a mound which – according to atmospheric conditions may dry evenly or unevenly.

A dot requires good circumstances for manifestation or "growth"
It requires sun to dry, and water to emerge,
combined with creative hand.

If there is too much water in the paint, the dot may run, and then it is up to painters – creators – to stop that flow before it messes up a different part of the painting. They will react immediately and soak up the extra fluid with a cloth.

If the dot is too turgid, with a thick crust, it can sometimes be removed with a knife. If an overall harmonious effect is to be achieved, then all dots must be equal.

If the painter is not concentrated, then the dot may be malformed.

If the brush is stubby or damaged,
a perfect dot cannot be formed.

If there is not enough light to see, if twilight is approaching or if the sun has not yet risen, then there is the danger of making imprecise and inappropriate dots because the contours and colour contrasts are not fully visible.

If the painter is distracted by fear, worry, sadness, burdens or even hedonistic musings, then concentration will be broken, and it will not be so easy to continue and create the dots one wishes.

If you paint dots for too long, or if the colours are too intense or contrasting, the painter's eyes will start to water and vision will become blurred, and then you will not be able to continue painting for a while, depending on the severity of the symptoms.

It may be helpful to you to contemplate yourselves as the painter, attempting to create something beautiful, balanced and worthy. It may be helpful to consider the dots as your creations, however small or humble, which are generated as a result of your thoughts and actions.

In the action of painting dots, averaging one dot a second as does this scribe, it is necessary to concentrate fully. A second of thoughtlessness or distraction will have immediate negative results. Your thoughts function in a similar way. If you allow them to constantly roam aimlessly, they will result in an aimless life, and what you manifest as a result will be random and uncoordinated. If you are aware of your thoughts and their creative power in every second, your manifestations will be grandiose.

We cannot emphasise enough THE POWER OF YOU.

And so, this is not only an ode to the dot, but to you also, for small seeds planted by you consciously with constant dedication can have enormous effect.

You may ask: what powerful things can dots do? Dots can separate light from dark. They can crystallise into new forms, and can define edges. They can brighten or darken. They can correct and balance. They are individual but they can have a collective effect. They are individual but if they are very close together or overlapping then they create on homogenous surface. They can break up already existing patterns and create new structures. In short, they are powerful agents of change if placed in the right position with concentrated intent.

This is your task, Beloveds, at a time when you may consider yourselves helpless. Know your importance and that you can contribute to massive change.

Seraphin

Seraphin Message 541
METAMORPHOSIS AND THE PARTING OF THE MIST

Through Rosie, 18th October 2023

When you think of metamorphosis, Beloveds, most of you will reflect upon the truly astonishing examples of metamorphosis in nature, when a snake throws off its skin, when a caterpillar turns into a butterfly, and when a tadpole turns into a frog. Tadpoles and caterpillars appear miraculously capable of producing and immediately using new limbs or accoutrements in new environments previously unattainable – water to land, land to air. These developments are "part and parcel" of their lives, as you see it.

YET YOU ARE ALSO PART OF NATURE AND
CAPABLE OF SIMILAR TRANSFORMATIONS!
Just as a tadpole and caterpillar are programmed to develop,
SO ARE YOU!

The only difference being that you will be familiar with the whole process in every detail, following every small change, following through on the relationship between cause and effect at every stage.

There will be times, especially now, when you feel stagnant and paralysed, despairing of the fact that nothing will ever change, resigned to the fact that the world is in inextricable chaos and that no one is going to change their opinions, their strategies and – most importantly – their greed and belligerence.

However, it is of the essence that you CONTINUE TO MOVE FORWARD, if only in baby steps, SO THAT MILLIONS OF BABY STEPS CAN HAUL THE GREAT WAR MACHINE OUT OF THE MUD. Imagine yourselves pulling such a machine out of the mud with thousands of others.

Putting your shoulders to the wheel AT THE SAME TIME AND WITH CONTINUOUS EFFORT will have an effect.

Once you have control of the movements of the machine, you also have control of its next action, or lack of action. You can turn it around to fire back, thus perpetuating violence, or you can set it on automatic and point it towards the edge of a steep cliff. Together you can achieve anything. This is why it is so important that you small movements continue, in a direction which serves humanity.

Spectacular changes can be achieved – a complete metamorphosis in fact – as a result of myriad small decisions and forward movements. This is equivalent to the cells of the frogs, growing daily to form legs, or to the cells of the butterflies, growing daily to form new wings, even if this is a long and unseen process.

The second part of the title of this piece concerns the "mist that parts". Many of you are afflicted by "mind fog", which is partly resignation to being flooded with incongruities, noise, discrepancies or horrors, all of which serve to make your brains stop working, for it is all indistinguishable and cannot be understood. Thus you are in closed down mode.

The "dark side" has used several methods very successfully over many years, centuries and millennia, to burden your thinking processes and turn you into unquestioning automatons. This is on the physical level, concerning substances in food and in the air, as well as psychological ruses and general overstimulation with useless distractions and harmful suggestions.

IN FACT, THERE IS LITTLE NEED ANY MORE TO FEED THIS TO YOU, BECAUSE MUCH IS ALREADY ASSIMILATED AND YOU OBEY AUTOMATICALLY.

Like a wound-up mechanical toy, you are set to move in one certain direction only. That is their goal, and your lives are controlled.

However, incoming "waves" or positive energy from beyond your tiny planet are presently carrying out a sorting process. They are able to pierce through the fog, blasting it away.

PREPARE TO HAVE A SUDDEN AND UNRESTRICTED VIEW.

This also means the clearing away of all uncertainties which have been the source of great fear. It also means the revealing of many hitherto hidden constructs, intentions and control mechanisms. You will be presented with the unadulterated truth. It will be like trudging through a dark misty night, carrying an immeasurably heavy burden, without any hope of ever seeing the light of day, to the clouds suddenly parting and being blinded by the brightest light you have ever seen in your life.

You will notice that I did not say that your burden would be taken from you. Your burdens are your own. If you decide that they are no longer necessary, then you can discard them at any stage. If you are the "worrisome" type, with no faith in the divine plan, then you will hold on to your worries despite anything which happens around you. By the same token, you can blithely dance through these times of darkness without any burdens whatsoever, though we do advise a degree of watchfulness and awareness, for the darkness has not yet come to an end, and there will be unexpected "surprises" or "developments" which may cause you to take a step backwards.

The thing is: ALWAYS KEEP TWO FEET ON THE GROUND and try to keep a clear head, despite all the stories and attempts to confuse you. We are accompanying you on this difficult path.

Know that it will end. Seraphin

Seraphin Message 542
THE BELL TOLLS FOR THEE

Through Rosie, 28th Oct. 2023

Dearly beloved inhabitants of earth: with tensions rising daily, if not hourly, on your planet, you may or may not be aware of the devastating consequences of the mounting violence. You may be located in a safe, remote area, watching all the videos (whether true or faked) with rising dread, yet you may still consider this scenario as something SEPARATE FROM YOURSELVES.

Let us be quite clear about this, so that you realize and internalize this once and for all:

NOTHING IS SEPARATE FROM YOURSELVES.

Similarly, everything and every situation is a clear indication of your spiritual maturity, or lack of it. In view of the warmongering and violence it is likewise clear that your global level of spiritual maturity is very low.

As always, we are trying to draw attention to your collective and individual responsibility. If individuals are really in charge of their emotions and practice integrity, diligence, dedication and sincere self-reflection daily, then the collective result is

INDESTRUCTIBLE PEACE.

Yet still, you may brush off all this and state that you are not involved. EVERYONE is involved in the burden which your earth, Gaia, presently carries, and believe me, she wishes to throw off this burden, having served you all with great dedication for so long, yet she has now come to the end of her tether.

So, it is time for everyone to review their lives, as if you only have a short time to live. This is in fact the case for many of you. I repeat; many only have a short time to sort yourselves out. We recommend going into meditation and reviewing your life, including assessing your behaviour and your moral standards, determining when you acted in a way which was less than par and destructive to others.

We are not talking huge events only. We are talking small daily habits too, because everything counts. This is the sort of assessment process which follows your release from your physical body in death, and indeed this will be your experience if you refuse to do it now. We sound harsh but we speak to you out of love. - Seraphin

Seraphin Message 543
THE HEALING ROOM 3

Through Rosie, 6th Nov. 2023

Dearest inhabitants of earth; following this period of depravity and destruction, the time will come for NEW CONSTRUCTS AND NEW CONSTRUCTIONS. Your planet will, in effect, become a global healing room, not only for the benefit of Gaia and for all those remaining on her soil, but as an EXAMPLE to other planets which have fallen into similar states of distress. Instead of exemplifying EXTREME DARKNESS, Earth will become a SHINING LIGHT of inspiration regarding how to defeat the adversary which - as you will clearly begin to see - takes all sorts of forms, including forms which initially appear to be undoubtedly positive. Discovery and revelation of such will indeed be shocking to many, and many will not survive this shock because it will shatter all familiar and well-loved parameters. They will not be able to bear - mentally and emotionally - the degree of change in perception which is necessary to continue functioning physically.

When your planet is a global healing room, there will not be any DIRTY, MESSY OR DERELICT CORNERS, and we would ask you to try and visualise what this actually means. This is a concept which applies on all levels. On the physical level, it means assuming responsibility for all derelict corners, where no growth can presently take place, and thus where no healing processes can ensue.

You will be the GUARDIANS of every city, every river, and all physical spaces. When the Earth is a global healing room (and we assure you that this is an obligatory step after so much deviant behaviour and actions throughout millennia) every space must become surveyed, protected, and made holy. There will be no more ruins, dumps or wastelands of rubbish.

In the end,
EVERY ROOM IN EVERY BUILDING
WILL BECOME A HEALING ROOM.

Perhaps you think we are exaggerating, BUT NO!

This is necessary for the well-being and growth of all. It means great attention to cleanliness and detail, coupled with a deep desire to go forth and create something sacred and beautiful.

Can a factory or a toilet or a hospital become a sacred place?
OF COURSE, and you can make it so.

A worldwide global healing room project will be initiated (as described by this scribe) in order to serve as inspiration; those who are creative will inspire those who think they are not creative.

We would also like to remind you that when we say that every space will become sacred (resulting from individual and collective effort) then this includes ALL THE SPACES IN YOUR MINDS and all the spaces in your BODIES. To cram such spaces with mindless poisons will be unthinkable. To refuse to take care of bodily spaces such as your oral cavity, your blood cells or your bone apparatus et cetera et cetera will be unthinkable. In the true global healing room, contamination of such, or negligence of such, will not be contemplated or tolerated.

In short, you will strive for excellence in every sphere, not in order to impress or gloat, as is now often the case with those who excel (without attention to their physical form, we might say, thus producing stress and disease) but in order to raise the general level of sacredness so that everyone can benefit, including yourselves.

We know that it is difficult to dream of such when wars reign on your world, producing unprecedented levels of tension, whether you are intensely aware of this or not. Yet we encourage you to take breaks in your watchfulness to dream on, for just as a pregnant woman focuses on birth, you are focusing on the future rebirth of your world, yet all of a sudden, the birth will be over and then you will find yourselves in completely new circumstances where your action is required.

We ask you not to neglect these more expansive perspectives while over focusing on the imminent birth.

We know that some of you have an aversion to words such as 'imminent' or 'soon', yet we assure you that the process of cause and effect never fails and your joint actions have led you to the point of no return.

You will inevitably see and experience the consequences
as soon as the balloon bursts.

We love you, Seraphin

Seraphin Message 544

EXPECT EXPLOSIONS

Through Rosie, 16th November 2023

Some of you who are reading here have been undergoing a sort of shock therapy treatment initiated by yourselves. You live with intent, and with determination, forging ahead, searching out material or background information which is indeed shocking beyond all "norms".

Why have you done this?

Because you see depravity everywhere. You want to investigate the roots of this thoroughly in order to prevent it. You want to take preventive measures, which means delving deep below the surface rather than dealing with never-ending symptoms. Some of the symptoms are shocking enough, yet to reach further down is much worse. What you encounter may paralyse you initially, but for those in whom conscience plays a strong role, it is so perverse and nauseating that you continue undeterred in the hope of alleviating pain permanently.

This is what we of the angelic hosts are aiming for on a worldwide scale: the permanent eradication of pain, which means the permanent eradication of the CAUSES OF THE PAIN. It does not mean increasing leniency of that which subdues the pain, such as drugs and alcohol. We understand why these are being used, and we have compassion for the users, but this is not a permanent solution and many thereby go down the path of no return, rejecting their divine potential and refusing to acknowledge their own very great significance.

Thus there are people who deliberately seek out the "shocks", of which there are many, in order to solve problems permanently, and also in order to have information at their fingertips to forward to others, if it can be accepted.

Some of you may be able to accept that you have been lied to continuously, if you are steadily drip-fed with snippets of information (smaller shocks) allowing you to form your own composite picture of the situation with time.

YET TIME IS RUNNING OUT, and so the shocks are now increasing in size and in pace of exposure. All this results in great tension, sadness and anger so that you may feel that you want to explode. It remains to be seen how each individual will cope with this, or indeed to see whether they can cope at all.

In addition to this internal process which will require great growth from each individual, the external process will act out in parallel. Internal tension is not only present in yourselves BUT ALSO IN THE BODY OF YOUR EARTH, GAIA, and so you will inevitably feel her strivings to adjust, to rebalance, and to free up new learning territory.

Imagine yourselves exploding with frustration and anger. Earth will do the same. This will take the form of shaking and moving and venting, manifesting on her skin as quakes, earth movements and volcanic eruptions. Now more than ever, it is time to realise that she is a sentient being undergoing a similar journey to yourselves. She does not wish to be abused or paralysed, any more than you do. She will scream, as you will. As you also, she will wish to move forward IN HER OWN TRUTH TO FULFIL HER OWN POTENTIAL, USING HER FULL CAPACITIES. This is a forewarning of the explosions to come, Seraphin

Seraphin Message 545

YOUR INEXTINGUISHABLE LIGHT WITHOUT A DEADLINE

Through Rosie, 4th December 2023

Those who are aware that there is something "unreal" and monumental going on in their world, and on their planet, will automatically thirst for more information. They will want to know, foremost, WHEN THIS MADNESS WILL END so that suffering generally – and their suffering individually – will cease.

We hear you and respond to this lovingly with the following: as much as we would like to respond to this fervent desire to know more, we are not enabled to provide details, although we can see very clearly, from our viewpoint, the "domino pieces" which have been put in line, and which are destined to fall one after another. We can see the hardships that you in the "know" endure, and we gravely regret that we cannot provide you with a message of that nature, for this would set off processes which, in the end, would have negative responses or effects, to say nothing of the learning opportunities missed.

Know that we are ever progressing towards our mutual goal, which is the denouement of all which is evil, to be fully laid out in front of your very eyes, to the winding down of this planetary phase on your earth, leading to future renewal. In this, many of you will play a major role.

However, instead of a message with details and dates, we can provide you with a message of hope. Even in the depths of darkness and oblivion, there is always hope. You may not see any light whatsoever around you, BUT THERE IS ALWAYS A LIGHT

INSIDE YOU, and this is independent of any incarnation you happen to be in, any planet you happen to be on, and any grave situation which threatens. It is radiating this light outwards which makes you a beacon of hope for others. Thus, you can all work together in these dark times. Your light is inextinguishable, even through death, if you choose to align yourselves with godly purposes, and these are great in variety. Your dedication is so desperately needed on a sphere of darkness such as this.

On the other hand, it is necessary to "retire" temporarily from the scene, if it is clear to you that nothing can be done. In this case, celestial hand will take over, for there is nothing it cannot achieve. Thus, you are never "lost", Beloveds. You are simply on another path which has not yet turned the bend. You are simply not yet on the brow of the hill which will provide you with a new horizon. And this new horizon will also be provided by celestial hand.

We hope that we have been able to give you some respite concerning your musings and your worry about how all this is going to end. There are so many people who say "This can't end well", and in a way, they are completely correct.

The other side of the coin is that the more a situation becomes absurd, and the more it becomes obvious that something does not add up, and the more the violence appears to be "senseless", THE MORE PEOPLE COME TO THEIR SENSES, and this is a major aim in consideration of the work which has to be done next.

We hold you in our arms and in our thoughts constantly on this final leg.

Seraphin

Seraphin Message 546

CELEBRATING THE CHRIST

Through Rosie, 11th December 2023

Due to poor, inconsistent, irrelevant, incomplete and deliberately manipulative teaching, most inhabitants on your earth have been left swirling in a muddy whirlpool of discoloured "waters of truth", with no idea of how you could actually immerse yourselves in the crystal-clear waters of healing.

Why do we use this imagery? Because water is a very powerful agent of cleansing if unsullied, capable of effecting physical BUT ALSO SPIRITUAL RENEWAL, and it is the latter which is so needed on your planet. All else follows.

The Christ, the one you refer to as Jesus (as well as other "masters") was well aware of this potential and of the healing properties of water as a cleaning agent and information carrier.

This is all about UNSULLIED INFORMATION, Beloveds, yet your minds need to be "reconfigured" in order to best accept and integrate it. Your world with its rituals, superstitions and other mental constructs, all supported by physical "rules" (or should we say "prisons"), present you with certain damaged information parameters which serve to keep you intimidated, fearful, and always seeking security. Thus new information – however radical or "earth-changing" in a positive sense, will not find a way into your brains, In fact, it will not even be considered. It will simply be dismissed out of hand. We consider this to be the true "brain-fog" afflicting the majority.

The "missing information" which could change the world for the better is THAT YOU HAVE THE CAPACITY TO BECOME CHRISTS. This means, in fact, that when you celebrate the

Christ, YOU SHOULD BE CELEBRATING THE CHRIST IN YOURSELVES. Neither should this be limited to a "once a year" experience. Neither does it have anything to do with excessive consumption or excessive present-giving. It has nothing to do with "living it up", getting drunk or contributing to conflict. This may surprise you, but there are more family conflicts and tears during your holiday period than at any other time of the year.

To increase your own Christ-like qualities and be intensely aware of your own potential daily, is not a desecration of Christmas:

IT IS AN AUGMENTATION OF IT,
for the Christ was a way shower FOR YOU,
and it is worthy to celebrate
THIS SERVICE TO YOU.

To best honour his work is to follow his behaviour as closely as possible in every second. Again, it has nothing to do with a meaningless annual repetition of Christmas lights and office parties.

You will see that we are mainly addressing the planet's "western" and "Christian" population here, but we assure you that the message of the Christ applies worldwide and that his behaviour and principles should be adopted worldwide as a

TEMPLATE FOR PEACE,
IRRESPECTIVE OF RELIGIOUS PERSUASION
OR AFFILIATION.

The brutal conflicts characterising your world at the moment, and which have done for millennia are proof
THAT YOU HAVE NOT YET LIVED YOUR INNER CHRIST.

You will be asked to make a choice – of YES OR NO – as to whether your heart is open to this particular path, or whether you intend to continue to block it off.

Christ's intention – like the intentions of all the messengers who have come to your earth – was for you to become THE LIGHT OF THE WORLD, like himself.

This is indeed your last chance. It is time to be about this business, just as the Christ often stipulated that he was about his father's business.

We spur you on today to become that population of Christ-like beings through determined action, rather than to sink into the temporary frivolities of your Christmas celebrations. Seraphin.

Seraphin Message 547

BEYOND THE WALL

Through Rosie, 28th December 2023

Dearly Beloveds on earth: when we see what a predicament you are in – mostly completely unbeknown to yourselves – we are very moved emotionally and deeply saddened. Indeed, the saddest part is that you do not realise it yourselves. You continue blithely without a worry in the world, or continue in a depressed and resigned manner, aware perhaps that things are not "in order", or that there may be horror scenarios playing out somewhere, but you are majorly relieved that it is not playing out right in front of your own front doors.

We may remind you that those experiencing war and poverty and abuse directly do have the luxury of such thoughts. Neither do they have the choice of "believing" or "not believing". They are faced with reality and the truth, at least within the perimeters of their own suffering.

There will come a time in the near future when all perimeters will be scaled. Imagine that you are wandering around aimlessly in the dark and wondering how to get out of a forest you have stumbled into. You suddenly see a wall in front of you, and you follow the wall, hoping to find a door which will enable your escape.

After hours of following the wall, you realise that you have arrived at your place of departure. (This represents your imprisonment of mind in a structure which you cannot break out of, if you just diligently follow what seems to be like the most likely path presented to you). To get out of this situation, it is necessary to have a NEW IDEA. You remember a ladder which was lying beneath the undergrowth. You retrieve it and set it against the wall, all the time stumbling through the undergrowth in near pitch darkness.

When you climb the ladder, you can suddenly see BEYOND THE WALL. You are greeted with a BURST OF LIGHT, with a huge and impressive NEW HORIZON, with facts and experiences which you have never seen before. This is the hour of reckoning and of "enlightenment", if you choose it, and if you choose – in circumstances of great difficulty – to climb the ladder.

What you will see and learn will - in one huge jolt - take your breath away. If you are not holding onto the ladder with all your might, you may fall off. You may feel weak at the knees in recognition of the fact that you have been deceived, that you have succumbed to evil, that you have failed to discern the iron-like grip that the "dark side" has exercised over you and in fact over the majority for millennia. Your small worries and concerns will pale in view of all this. You will consider huge perspectives, eternal values, expansive solutions. Your mind will either EXPLODE with new ideas, or it will not be able to cope. This will be the most difficult challenge of your lives.

You will of course ask WHEN WILL ALL THIS HAPPEN?

And we say that the preparations for this have been ongoing FOR MILLENNIA ALSO, and that it will soon come to pass. For you, it may be a sudden revelation, but for us it is the inevitable culmination of years of preparation. For some, it will come as a sigh of relief, but irrespective of whether you have been anticipating it or not, you are in for a shock. It will be a severe test of your ability to react in adverse circumstances, and to recognize the good which will come of them.

We cannot now describe what is going to happen. It is our mission to inform you and to warn you of the severity of the situation, whether you are prepared or not. This preparation is mostly mental and spiritual, though it will also help to be physically prepared as in stocking up on various provisions.

It is our motive to make you aware. We do not wish to instill fear, though a message of this nature may have this effect.

The challenge is to move away from emotions which instantly arise – like fear – and to focus on the question of

WHAT CAN I DO NOW? HOW CAN I BE OF SERVICE?

This is what it all boils down to, before and after this event, before and after you climb the wall.

We would also recommend the story called THE ROOF*, written by this scribe, which well illustrates the experience of living an enclosed life without knowing what happens beyond the wall. You are under our protection, Seraphin

* THE ROOF

There was once a concrete city with very few green areas, and the whole district was covered by a roof and sealed off from the exterior by thick walls. The inhabitants were small, stunted humans who stooped and walked slowly, their eyes turning to the ground in great humility, as if they recognised having committed a major crime and were doing everything in their power to make amends. And indeed, it was the general consensus that they HAD actually committed a crime of great proportions, for their leaders had built the roof over their heads to protect them from the air which had been polluted and poisoned by all sorts of human actions and waste products.

For this, all inhabitants were genuinely sorry. They realised that they had collectively destroyed "nature", and that it was now their responsibility to nurture it. Thus, everyone was greatly encouraged to look after a number of pot plants, sending them love every day. Those with knowledge about plants warned that these remaining species were also severely weakened, and that they would not survive strong exposure to light, and would suffer from over-watering and from repotting.

Sometimes the inhabitants would take their pot plants for a walk. If they wished to venerate their pot plants, they would take them to the GARDEN OF NATURE ADORATION where – it was felt – there was a higher vibration due to the accumulation of plants. At the very centre of the garden was the trunk of an enormous tree. The inhabitants were given to understand that the tree was now dead but that it had once been a flourishing example of "nature" in the old days, when everything was still intact and when the air was still pure.

Every day, people would pour into the garden bearing their pot plants, remembering the once glorious tree, admitting their guilt and stating their intent to make amends. They prayed and sang, determined to do their very best to rectify their wrong. They were determined to live humbly, with few possessions and demands, for the collective good. They praised and thanked their leaders for building the roof at a very critical period in their history so long ago, which had preserved their existence and which had avoided the complete obliteration of their species.

The huge tree trunk was surrounded by a circular bench. Here, residents were allowed to sit in reverence and silent meditation, holding their pot plants on their knees. Citizens who did this often developed a certain sensitivity. They noticed that strong energy was emanating from the trunk of the tree. They felt it in their backs as a tingling sensation. This was very disturbing, to say the least, as it had been maintained for centuries that the tree was DEAD. It would have amounted to sacrilege to mention this to anyone else, yet the dedicated group of people who noticed this - and who were able to trust each other with their reservations and feelings - met daily at the tree. They nodded to each other and knew intuitively (as the tree had awakened their intuitive abilities) that they were all aware of the same phenomenon - of the secret power of the tree.

These people were – in turn – observed by watching officials. One day, a fence was put up around the tree trunk to prevent people from approaching it closely. The sign said that the fence was necessary "TO BETTER PRESERVE OUR ANCIENT HERITAGE AND IN RECOGNITION OF OUR GUILT AND NEED TO DO PENANCE". Most visitors nodded their heads sadly in agreement. But the group of sensitives had different feelings. They were forced to go "underground" to discuss what was going on. They did this literally, meeting in an old disused cellar. And it was here that they discovered a piece of TREE ROOT emerging from the wall.

After careful examination and experimentation, they pronounced this to be the living root of a living tree. Secretly, they watered the root, which drank it up immediately, as if suffering from a hundred years of thirst. The group continued to feed the root and to encourage the tree to GROW. This in itself would have been considered heresy, as the general rule for pot plants was QUICK GROWTH WILL KILL. Thus "repotting" was against the rules. The idea that a pot plant needed "repotting" was condemned as harmful superstition.

And so, the root grew. When the group visited the garden, they noticed hair cracks in the paving, and they looked at each other with knowing glances. The cracks widened daily, and soon there was another notice which said: "THE GARDEN IS TO BE PRESERVED AS A MONUMENT TO NATURAL BEAUTY, AND CAN THEREFORE NO LONGER BE EXPOSED TO DETRIMENTAL HUMAN CONTACT AND POLLUTION". Most visitors nodded sadly when they saw this sign, and they stood at the locked gates and sent love to the garden.

But still the roots continued to grow. On the streets, cracks started to appear, and road maintenance swiftly became very busy "CORRECTING STRUCTURAL DAMAGE DUE TO DISREPAIR". But this was so widespread that it was impossible to hide or suppress any longer. People wandering through the streets were astonished to find plants and bushes suddenly sprouting through the pavement. This was truly wondrous for those who stopped long enough to feel the beautiful uplifting energy which emanated from the plants. Others rushed away in fright, for this was an impossible phenomenon which did not fit into their worldview.

Officials attempted to eliminate the bushes during the darkness of night, but with time, they were observed by the inhabitants, some of whom broke down to see such beauty being destroyed.

They could not understand why officials were desecrating the nature which they had so long been protecting, or so they said.

Chaos ensued. The roots were now fully visible and growing at a tremendous rate, especially as the group of sensitives was now openly encouraging the inhabitants to provide them with water, and the response grew by the hour. Buildings were starting to collapse. Some rejoiced in this fantastic development which showed them that nature was truly ALIVE IN ALL ITS GLORY, AND OTHERS LAMENTED THE DESTRUCTION OF THEIR HOMES. THEY CURSED THE ROOTS AND HACKED THEM OFF WHEREVER THEY COULD. BUT THERE WAS NO POINT IN THIS, AS THE GROWTH MOMENTUM WAS SO GREAT. ONE ROOT CUT OFF WAS REPLACED BY SEVEN.

IN THE END, THE VERY ROOF OVER THEIR HEADS BEGAN TO CRACK. When they noticed this, crowds of citizens stormed the gates of their huge, roofed compound, overthrowing the guards who kept watch, and burst beyond the perimeters of their known world, expecting to be met by poisoned air and bare, blackened countryside.

But instead of this, the people discovered lush, abundant fields, and as they looked back at their former grey concrete home, they saw the huge tree at its centre. It was very much alive, and its enormous green crown stretched high into the sky.

It was then that the people realised that they had been

SLAVES FOR CENTURIES, LIVING A LIE,
SUBDUED BY FALSELY ACCREDITED GUILT,
ALLOWING THEIR RULERS TO LIVE
IN PARADISE AND ABUNDANCE,
WHILE THEY THEMSELVES HAD LIVED IN POVERTY
WITHIN THE WALLS OF THEIR PRISON.

Seraphin Message 548
THE LAST BATTLE BEFORE THE NEW ERA

Through Rosie, 8th January 2024

Do you feel as if you are in a BATTLE, Beloveds?

If you do not, then we assure you that it is only a matter of time. While the battles taking place physically on your earth at this time are very serious and damaging in a way you cannot currently imagine, you will find that the INNER BATTLES IN YOURSELVES will take an even greater toll in the sense that they will be ALL CONSUMING AND CONSTANT until you have found a way to deal with them.

Some people will definitely not be able to cope, and you may see signs of "madness" or you may see those who are dangerously out of control. Your mandate is to help the former and defend against the latter. While these battles may express themselves on a physical level, they will be the result of inner turmoil (this is actually always the case, but even more poignant now).

What will this inner turmoil be? The discrepancy between what you thought was happening and what is happening in reality. The discrepancy between who you thought was honourable, honest and trustworthy, and the scoundrels, abusers and criminals that they turn out to be (AND VICE VERSA! Some of your so-called criminals are actually angels).

To continue: the discrepancy between your very firmly held beliefs and treasured memories and the fictitious, superstitious fragments of experience they turn out to be. The discrepancy between your priorities so far and the Divine mandate you failed to follow. Major revelations will clarify your view.

Is this already enough for you, Beloveds? But actually, we have only mentioned a few of the more "broad-brush" scenarios. There will be myriad small scenarios, and severe disappointments, and sudden realisations, all of which will shatter your present reality on a very individual and personal level, according to how you have lived, what stances you have taken (or not taken), what choices you have made and what "influencers" (in the widest sense of the word) you have chosen to follow.

You may feel immensely weary. You may realise that your life was worthless up to this point because you have involved your-selves in activities which have benefitted the adversary. You may feel that life is not worth living any more. You may be filled with shame. You may want to end your life. But we say that

EVERYTHING LEADING TO THIS POINT
IS OF EXTREME VALUE IN THE SENSE THAT IT HAS
FORCED THE MAJOR RECOGNITION THAT YOU WERE
TRAVELLING IN THE WRONG DIRECTION.

THE JOY IN THIS IS THAT YOU CAN NOW CHOOSE
TO GO IN A NEW DIRECTION,
ARMED WITH HONESTY, KINDNESS, COMPASSION
AND NEW KNOWLEDGE ABOUT DIVINE LAW
AND THE CELESTIAL OBSERVANCE OF SAME.

THERE WILL BE A RECONNECTION TO THE CELESTIAL HIERARCHY WHICH IS INVOLVED IN THIS FINAL CLOSING STAGE IN THE PLANET'S HISTORY, AND THEY WILL BE THE BRINGERS OF "GOOD NEWS", THE HARBINGERS OF BETTER THINGS TO COME AND THE ROLE MODELS YOU HAVE ALL BEEN WAITING FOR.

Thus, you have the choice of giving up and dying in shame be-cause your ego refuses to give way, or you can pick yourselves up and travel a new path. In many ways, this new path will be a great relief. You will no longer encounter deceivers, exploiters or thieves. You will no longer be fighting a battle to understand what is going on, because EVERYTHING WILL BE TRANSPARENT. You will no longer be governed by monsters. You will no longer face a new morning with a grim look of resignation. You will no longer spend your time in pursuits of money or in pursuit of trivial and worthless pastimes.

Instead, you will rejoice that you are now
in the company of travelers

OF THE SAME MIND,
WITH THE SAME GOALS,
SHARING THE SAME DISAPPOINTING HISTORY,
BUT ALSO SHARING THE STUPENDOUS GOALS
WHICH WILL PROPEL YOU INTO A NEW ERA OF JOY,
PROSPERITY AND PEACE –
A PEACE WHICH MEANS
AN END TO ALL BATTLES.

Will you plunge into this icy water, Beloveds,
knowing that it will turn into a
warm and comforting bath?

If so, you will become invigorated and
even more ready to welcome the new.

We embrace you as you travel through these "icy climes"
on the last leg of this period.

Seraphin.

Seraphin Message 549

INCREASING MOMENTS OF CLARITY

Through Rosie, 17th January 2024

Do you know, Inhabitants of Earth, what it genuinely means to see clearly? Have you ever, in fact seen anything in a clear, unbiased way? Though you may be convinced that this is something you have always strived for on your learning journey, as you increase in discernment, know that there is such an enormous counteraction taking place – and which has been ongoing for ages past – that it is literally impossible for you to see in absolute clarity, or to discern the pure and unadulterated truth.

You may have a sudden insight, and you may shriek

EUREKA! I HAVE DISCOVERED SOMETHING
SO NEW AND MEANINGFUL
THAT I AM THROWN INTO A STATE OF EUPHORIA.

But this euphoria is short-lived because of the very nature of your way of living and due to the very nature of the adversary.

To see clearly is to be IN A CONSTANT STATE OF EUPHORIA, because you can see all the results of any one choice, and you are always in a position to make the right choice, if guided by cosmic law which states that everything should be for the benefit of humanity, and of course this benefits you as a member.

Thus, your clear, euphoric moments are – at the moment – just moments. They may be ecstatic but short-lived – and many on earth tend to turn to drugs to gain a similar (but in actual fact vastly inferior) effect for a longer period. As a general rule in your warped and distorted world, moments of insight or enlightenment are rare in an environment where there are so many distractions and efforts to ensure the opposite.

As things progress towards the final denouement, there will be an unravelling of all threads of misleading information which have been deceiving you for so very long, and these moments of clarity will increase in size and severity. Unfortunately, they will come over as more of a shock than a marvelous revelation, for as we have already said, you have been successfully trained to accept untruths.

Let us take an example: if you are estranged from a friend because they turned into a "conspiracy theorist", and if you discover that this person has actually always been sincere, always attempting to warn you, always coming from a place intending to benefit you, and that they are actually in every instance RIGHT ABOUT EVERYTHING THEY SAID, then you will be practically "SMACKED IN THE FACE" by HOW WRONG YOU WERE, and you will hang your heads in shame. You will want the ground to swallow you up quickly.

Yet we say that although this is a shock,
it is essential to continue to KEEP YOUR EYES WIDE OPEN,
AVIDLY SEARCHING FOR MORE OF THE SAME MOMENTS,
for to do otherwise would be to
RETIRE FROM REALITY AND TO GIVE UP,
to sully the vision of others rather than
carrying the "sword and armour of God"
and deciding to propagate
THAT WHICH YOU FORMALLY ABHORRED.

Similarly, those who think they have done nothing wrong will be presented with undeniable proof of their wrongdoings. This will also be a shock to their system. And we ask them also to take a stand, publically admitting their crimes, thus providing the unsuspecting pubic with yet another "opportunity for discernment", another chance to open their eyes and develop their picture of what has actually be going on.

Will trauma ensure from all this?

That depends very much on the individual. Thus, we advise you to strengthen your inner connection, that is to say to the divine voice within yourself, which is only too ready to provide you with clear answers. But to hear them, you must be open, and if you are dithering around without any focus or direction, or if you are too ensconced in the physical and material world, such an inner voice will find no "SOUNDING BOARD".

Such is the struggle that we, of the unseen celestial realms, encounter when trying to get a message through to you. We see you stumbling – from one stumbling block to another – and in many cases, there is little we can do to prevent it simply because YOU DO NOT HEED OUR CALL.

We would ask you to please heed our call today. We would ask you that if you experience a revelation of truth or a moment of clarity, HOLD ONTO IT FOR DEAR LIFE. Write it down, proclaim it to the skies, reveal it to everyone you meet, and let it run like fire, illuminating one person after the other.

The alternative, which we do not support, is to extinguish it and to act as if you had never experienced it. Yet know that you will only be hit with it again, and the next time it will be harder until you can take it no longer.

You must assimilate and integrate these new ´truths" one by one, like a lengthy and well digested meal, instead of being force fed with masses of "food" ALL AT ONCE.

Some of you have assimilated new perspectives for many, many years. Others have focused purely on their everyday lives, but unbeknown to them there are countless real worlds beyond their experience and imagination.

Your world is presently overshadowed by the threat of war on many planes and in many countries. These are veritable storm clouds which instill great fear into the general public. Many are rendered immobile in their thinking structures and in their ability to feel universal compassion. Fear and shock serve to paralyse and divide. Polarisation will occur, resulting in fierce arguments about which side "deserves to win" or which side is "better". But one simple fact is overlooked: all conflicts have two aggressors. While there may be "justifiable reasons" for action, there is no point in determining which military is more justified to kill. There are no degrees of dead, just as there are no degrees of peace. You cannot have a "little bit of peace", just as you cannot have a "little bit of clarity".

You may consider us very strict, but when you CLEARLY SEE your terrible misdemeanors and deviations from the "moral road", you will realise why a very firm hand – a celestial hand we might add – will be necessary to rule your world.

We wish you a gradual development of clear insights and the ability to piece the puzzles together without losing hope.

Such insights should infuse you with the joy that you are "getting to the bottom" of things, which means that you are discovering the true causes of why your world has unfortunately been malfunctioning so far, and this is essential and necessary knowledge moving forward.

As many have said: THE STORM IS UPON YOU, but there is light between the clouds and it is up to you to search it out, to make sense of it, to join the dots, to rip away the false deterrents and the manufactured mistruths. WE ARE WATCHING YOU AS YOU MOVE TOWARDS THIS PAINFUL PROCESS WHICH IS DESTINED TO SPEED UP SHORTLY. Seraphin.

Seraphin Message 550
THE GREAT CHALLENGE AND THE GREAT OPPORTUNITY

Through Rosie, 24th January 2024

Imagine, Beloveds on Earth, that as you go about your daily life, there is an invisible string connecting your hand to the hand of your neighbour.

This means that when you shake the hand of someone else, your neighbour will feel the "pull" to do the same. If you water flowers, or if you hug your relatives, your neighbour will "feel" this and it will strengthen their own tendency to do the same.

The "downside" of this is that the neighbour's hand can also sense if you commit a crime with your hand, if you slap a child, if you waste amenities, if you curse continuously, or if you act in a violent manner. In this way, you are influencing your neighbour, encouraging deviant behavior. This gives a whole new meaning to the principle of LOVE THY NEIGHBOUR AS THYSELF, or rather, LOVE WHICH YOU DEMONSTRATE WILL ALSO REACH YOUR UNSEEN NEIGHBOUR.

Yet there is more. This connection between you and your neighbour, and with other neighbours, influences the quality of life in your environment or NEIGHBOURHOOD.

THIS MEANS THAT IN ORDER TO RAISE
THE VIBRATION OF YOUR NEIGHBOURHOOD,
YOU WOULD DO WELL TO REGULATE
YOUR BEHAVIOUR AND THOUGHTS,
ENSURING THAT THEY ARE
OF THE HIGHEST QUALITY.

Do you see how important this is, Beloveds?

Yet there is even more. You are not only connected to your neighbour BUT TO EVERYONE ON EARTH, in the sense that everyone is your neighbour, and you are all affecting each other for the better or worse, depending on your choices.

At this juncture, let us also mention that your "neighbours" include all "animals, vegetables and minerals" – in short – all cells on earth are affected by your very own personal thoughts which you thought were so private and which you have so far – for the most part – considered of little consequence.

BUT WE SAY TO YOU THAT THE CONSEQUENCES ARE HUGE, BEYOND YOUR IMAGINATION, AND BEYOND YOUR PLANET BECAUSE THE REST OF THE UNIVERSE IS POPULATED WITH YOUR NEIGHBOURS.

If you are conscious of just one connection – to your neighbour across the way - then a certain brotherly or sisterly relationship may develop. If you are conscious of the many neighbours in your town, there is a greater tendency that that town will flourish. The same applies to nations, countries and planets, extending even further to solar systems, galaxies, constellations, super universes and in fact the whole creation and ALL THAT IS.

This is one of the greatest challenges you will be faced with, because it involves

MINDFULNESS OF EVERY STEP AND EVERY INTENTION OF YOUR JOURNEY, IN THE FULL KNOWLEDGE THAT AS YOU MOVE, TRILLIONS OF BEINGS AND PLANETS MOVE WITH YOU, AND KNOWING THAT ONE POSITIVE OR NEGATIVE THOUGHT WHICH YOU SEND OUT INTO THE COLLECTIVE CONSCIOUSNESS CAN TIP THE BALANCE, CAN MAKE THE DIFFERENCE, CAN CAUSE UNIVERSES TO PLUNGE INTO DARKNESS OR TO SAIL INTO THE LIGHT.

We would like to end this message by emphasizing that every individual, therefore, possesses the great power TO DO GOOD, if they so choose, and we say also that a very poignant "period of choice" is now upon you. As always, you will determine your own future, both personal and collective.

Remember the truth of the phrase WHERE WE GO ONE WE GO ALL. YOU – AND WE OF THE CELESTIAL REALMS – ARE ALL INCLUDED IN THIS – THE SEEN WORLD AS WELL AS THE UNSEEN REALMS. Our love for our neighbours is extended to you, and we plead with you to develop the UNITY CONSCIOUS-NESS WHICH WILL TURN NOT ONLY YOUR PERSONAL ENVIRONMENT BUT ALSO YOUR WORLD AND YOUR UNIVERSE INTO AN ETERNAL PARADISE.

WE URGE YOU TO RECOGNISE THIS,
YOUR GREATEST OPPORTUNITY.
Seraphin

Seraphin Message 551

THE CENTRAL CELESTIAL UNIVERSE AND YOU

Through Rosie, 4th Feb 2024

Today, Beloveds, we would like to approach a topic which is very far away from your mind-frame or consciousness in an attempt to elevate you above the present turmoil which is increasingly "tightening" and becoming more acute on your earth plane.

We would ask you not to despair as "tragedies" unfold: it will be essential that you do not focus entirely on a given moment or place, but that you transcend such borders and allow ETERNITY and THE ETERNAL JOURNEY to be at the forefront of your minds, and thus the "dirty" and corrupt present will seem as an unpleasant but very necessary step towards what you would term, in your present surroundings and language, "a better life".

The Central Universe is celestial in nature as opposed to "temporary" or "human" or "lacking in moral integrity". (As you can see, we are making frequent use of inverted commas here since we can only touch on the qualities of the central universe using your limited language and concepts).

The Central Universe, far far away from your insignificant position at the edge of an outer constellation, is full of the brightest light you can imagine. One second of it would render you blind. One glimpse of such beauty would make you kneel on the ground in despair, knowing that it is the very antithesis of what you are presently experiencing. One note of celestial music would cure you forever and make you cry for weeks. There is no way we can actually describe all this other than to convey the incredible effect it would have on you, if experienced (and we would say that this juncture THAT THIS IS YOUR GOAL).

As a moth is attracted to the light,
YOUR SOUL IS ATTRACTED TO
THE GREATEST LIGHT OF ALL,
THE MOST SACRED SPACE,
THE SEAT OF THE MOST HOLY.

And we say that you are,
as small and as insignificant as you may view yourself,
A REFLECTION OF THIS LIGHT,
even though many rays be shattered or interrupted,
and even if the communication between the two is broken.

The central universe, like a distant, multi-coloured, magnificent disc or star, huge and multi-facetted and of the highest possible "love vibration", is connected to you as if by a thin thread travelling through space. This is tied to your inner divine core. This persists - unless you completely renounce the principles of the central universe – despite your sadness, your frustration, your pain, your present struggles. You can give the order to circulate healing energy through this circuit to assist you. Imagine yourself in a huge loop, to which you and the central universe are connected, and imagine light travelling continuously around it.

Heaven is the name you give to this.
Havona is the name we have used for this.
The seat of the Father, or the centre of Creation
are other designations for this.

Your planet has fallen into the "dark". This has been the case for many millennia. It has been an interminable struggle to develop from "animalistic tendencies" to enlightened human mind, and many have not succeeded in achieving this learning curve.

It requires total submission and surrender to Divine principles, and this is completely contrary to your surge towards "independence", "success" and material wealth – a direction which has sunk your world into a deep quagmire of abuse, corruption and violence.

To redress all this, your connection to the Divine must now be rekindled. Your alignment with erroneous concepts and damaging behaviours must end. Know that these will no longer be tolerated and that the experiment is over.

Recognise the increasing number of holes in the official narratives: watch the walls of your cages falling and a new consciousness rising and be determined to lead others out of their self-created "hell".

We are here to tell you that the Divine light of the Central Universe is always shining, always beckoning to you to come a little closer. Whatever happens, you can choose to fly like a butterfly or to continue on as a caterpillar. It is your choice. We love you and hope to strengthen your resolve and to inspire you to improve your very necessary connection to the Divine. Seraphin

Seraphin Message 552:

THE WINDS OF CHANGE WILL CARRY THOSE WHO FLY

Through Rosie, 17th February 2024

Is there reason to celebrate, Beloveds? (and in this regard, we refer you to the song text* just written by this scribe: and yes, we are involved in this, for singing is a way of releasing*).

On the surface of things as they presently stand, you appear to be surrounded by tragedies, chaos, violence and abuse.

Usually, it may take MANY YEARS to process such traumatic experiences which, when regarded with hindsight, you MAY be able to see things IN A DIFFERENT LIGHT. The prerequisite for this is a certain amount of self-reflection and an ability to "let go".

We say that this process will be "telescoped down" so that it is completed in a matter of days (Imagine an old-fashioned telescope which is fully extended, suddenly collapsing in on itself). This is a metaphor to illustrate the speed of change – and, most importantly, the change in your perception – which will occur.

There will be little opportunity to go into detail, to let your understanding of every step clarify and mature. You will be required to forgo all that – the measured "pace" which is personally chosen by yourselves for investigation, discernment and better comprehension. YOU WILL BE ON THE FAST TRACK! You will be confronted with facts and insights which you might have painfully extracted for yourselves after much time and effort, except that they will be facing you immediately and "head on". It will take a great leap of faith to expend with the interim phases and jump into this new "sea of truth".

Those who are not used to "jumping into cold water" (and there will be no other choice) will have a very hard time of it, and they may reject this sudden "cup of truth" as if it were poison. Yet to reject it means poisoning yourself in the sense that you remain immobile, immoveable, stagnant and – ultimately – dead. Yes, this refusal can indeed end in your demise, for it is your mandate to PROGRESS IN ACCORDANCE WITH DIVINE LAW, and if you refuse to "move on", and if you refute those laws, then there is no hope for you. We sound hard but we are actually only furnishing you with facts.

The law which is always in effect but which is manifesting results right now is the COSMIC LAW OF BALANCE. Can you see how your world is out of balance? Cosmic law stipulates that all imbalances must eventually be redressed, and that time is NOW.

To put it in a more pictorial way: too much violence, negativity and failure to act mindfully will impact the atmosphere negatively, just as your personal experience of same would negatively affect your own body and mental state. What would you do, if afflicted? You might cry and shout and flail around with your arms. This is what your earth does also, creating storms and wind which in turn wreak havoc on those where the violence ORIGINATED. Or you might bear it all, resigned to your fate, determined to show compassion whatever wrong doing you have suffered. This means that your bottled-up anger will inevitably surface at a later date, much like earth's bottled-up pressure which is emerging increasingly as explosive volcanoes and quakes.

In short, it is not possible to bear suffering indefinitely.
You will either submit completely (die) or revolt.
This is earth's position at the moment.

SHE IS MAKING A MAJOR ATTEMPT
TO REBALANCE HERSELF.

And because you live on her surface,
you will be presented with the consequences of this,
which in turn will force you to
REBALANCE YOURSELVES.

Therefore, we inform you about the very strong
WINDS OF CHANGE which are all but upon you.

Will you cower in the corners of your homes, Beloveds, refusing to contemplate that there is SO MUCH WHICH REQUIRES CLEANSING and SO MUCH WHICH NEEDS TO BE SWEPT OUT OF THE WAY?

Or will you venture outside, standing humbly but steadfastly in the wind, watching what atrocities are parading by, but knowing also that this is a precursor of something new and wonderful which does not include any of these negative things.

The question being:

WILL YOU TRY YOUR WINGS
AND REGAIN YOUR ABILITY TO FLY?
IF SO, THE WINDS OF CHANGE WILL CARRY YOU,
AND YOUR FLIGHT WILL BE COMPARATIVELY EASY.

This we ask you on the eve of great changes which will shatter your world view, the nature of your relationships, the constructs of your religions, and the false pretenses of almost all of the institutions and organisations with which you are familiar.

Instead, whole new structures, experiences and parameters based on DIVINE VALUES will appear overnight. It is up to you to leave the "old" behind and to march with determination towards the "new".

We are both excited and very apprehensive about how earth's present inhabitants will deal with this scenario. We fear that it will be "too much" for the majority. We entreat you to call on your inner guides for assistance. Seraphin.

CELEBRATION

A song by Rosie with celestial help

The tears have fallen
Faster than the rain
We are the Callen
Passing through the pain

And the winds of change will carry those who fly,
And the burdens we have carried quickly die

And learning how - the voice of the Divine
Will carry us – across the great divide

Celebrate the choices we made on the way
Celebrate heralding a new day
Celebrate the guidance that sits in our heart
Celebrate the sacred start

The faith was broken
Melting like the snow
Then truth was spoken
More than we could know

And the winds of change will carry those who cry,
And the sadness we have carried quickly die

And learning how the stories we have heard
Were all but lies – or heroes in disguise

Celebrate the closure of history past
Celebrate the new horizons so vast
Celebrate the visions of futures to be
Celebrate humanity

The age has fallen
Stumbling to the ground
Our hearts are open
More this time around

And the winds of change will carry those who fall,
And the weakness we have carried makes us tall

And learning how we fell into the fight
And came to know our aim is to unite

Celebrate the passion of new goals to come
Celebrate the world where we are all one
Celebrate the errors which brought a new start
Celebrate love in our heart

Seraphin Message 553:

THE DIRE CONSEQUENCES OF DENIAL OF IMPACT AND DENIAL OF CONTACT

Through Rosie, 23rd February 2024

With this impressive title, Beloveds on Earth,
we hope to bring your attention to your
PERSONAL POWER and your
PERSONAL SUPPORT SYSTEM.

If you are sitting in front of a dead tree, you may have a variety of experiences. In the abundance of the lush countryside, you may not even notice that the tree is dead. And you may not notice the countryside at all, in fact, because you may be shivering in a cold wind, or you are intent on finishing some task, or you are enthralled by some book, or you are mesmerized by the other worlds presented to you by your mobile phone, or because your head is full with seemingly insurmountable problems which spin around in constant circles of thought and worry.

In all these cases, the dead tree remains "untouched" and – to a great degree – unseen. Should there be a lull in your thinking processes, should there suddenly be a drastic change in "weather", should your phone no longer work, should there not be enough light to read, should a loud noise such as a cracking branch make you look up, then your gaze may well fall on the dead tree.

It is only then – if you are capable of it – that you might ask
WHY IS IT DEAD or
IS IT THE ONLY DEAD TREE? Or
IS IT TIME TO CUT IT DOWN? Or
WHAT HUGE VISTAS WILL IT REVEAL
ONCE IT HAS BEEN REMOVED?

Once your eye is focused on this, several "dead trees" may pop into view, not because they were not visible before, but because dead trees have now become your focus and have entered your conscious awareness.

Please take note of this process, because it is something which you will all go through on many levels. It will not be possible to ignore the increasing "icy winds" or the consequences thereof. It will not be possible to ignore the damage and the cries for help.

Nor will it be possible to ignore any more
ALL THAT WHICH IS VALUABLE WHICH HAS DIED.
The moment you "awake" to this,
the moment your mind is involved in this process,
the more you are
BLAZE TRAILING A LINE OF THOUGHT
FOR OTHERS TO FOLLOW.

You are carving out a track which makes it easier for others who are perhaps not so far developed in their thinking processes, allowing them to travel forward with more ease.

This means that everything you think,
everything you process, everything you learn,
and every step you take, is a
PIONEERING EXERCISE FROM WHICH
THE REST OF HUMANITY MAY PROFIT.

We realize that this may be a big statement to digest, but we assure you of the GREAT IMPACT OF YOUR EVERY ACTION.

And hand in hand with this goes your
GREAT RESPONSIBILITY.

So, if you are "in denial" that you have this impact (see title) the consequences are DIRE. You will think that a small misdemeanor here and there does not matter. But you deceive yourselves:

IT MATTERS GREATLY SINCE IT HAS A NEGATIVE IMPACT FAR BEYOND THE SCOPE OF YOUR COMPREHENSION, COLLECTIVELY CUMULATING IN VIOLENCE, WARS, ABUSE AND CORRUPTION.

You cannot pull away from this and say (DENIAL AGAIN!)
that you have no part in this,
FOR THE OUTCOME IS THE SUM OF ALL PARTS,
and you and all others are without a doubt
A SIGNIFICANT PART.

So much for our discourse on "the denial of impact".

We now move on to the "denial of contact". Do you imagine that we of the celestial realms, whose only intention is to love and guide you, would allow you to wander around hopelessly and helplessly without any help? We would say that the "hopeless" and "helpless" feelings which you harbour arise because you have cut yourselves off from us. You refuse to see us, just as you refuse to see the dead tree. You refuse to see the results of your actions – whether positive of negative – as connected to yourself, and you similarly refuse to acknowledge our existence.

This means ignoring the signs which we plant on your path to make you turn off in a different and less damaging direction – into a direction which is more beneficial to you and your world. This means rejecting the idea that you are here for a purpose, or that your life has a greater meaning. This means that we see you falter and wither away instead of being able to provide you with inspiration and sustenance which may come in the form of the next idea you receive or the next person you meet, who will always have a message for you.

We would like to give you a small but concrete example of this. At this very moment, this scribe is sitting in front of a dead tree, shivering a little because the wind is getting cold. A storm is on the way. As she began to write this message, she had no idea – apart from the title which we gave her earlier – what the message might contain. But as you can see, the tree and the wind have been "signposts" for her as to how this message should be got across to you. And an important message it is.

So, this is the sort of "contact" which is highly profitable for you at any stage of any task. You can of course completely ignore inner promptings (THE GOD WITHIN!) or outwards signs, but then you would be "in denial of contact", and this also, per the title, leads to dire consequences, for then we have no way of warning you or of preventing you cheerfully walking towards your complete demise.

Travel well dear friends, for the journey is still treacherous and you would do well to heed these inner voices which constitute your communication with the Divine. Seraphin.

Seraphin Message 554

TIED TO THE LAND: YOUR FATE AND FUTURE

Through Rosie, 1st March 2024

Today, Beloveds living presently on the planet you call EARTH, we have a significant question for you. Do you realise, in every cell of your being and in every corner of your soul, that your fate and the fate of your planet are intimately and intricately entwined, irrespective of time and space? Even when you have "moved on" to another planet, or another plane of existence, you will harbour

REMNANTS OF EARTH, not in the physical sense but in the sense that what you will have learnt here will remain in your memories and be utilized in order to teach others.

Notice that we say WHAT YOU WILL LEARN, because for some, the intense learning process has not yet begun, whereas for others, it started a long time ago. But irrespective of your position, you will continue learning.

We have recently told you
HOW TUMULTUOUS THE EFFECT WILL BE WHEN THE TRUTH IS FINALLY AND IRREVERSIBLY EXPOSED.

We do not say "the real truth" here, for truth in its very nature is real and complete. It can never be "partial", yet you have been exposed to some "smaller truths" which you may or may not have been able to take on board. Those have been attempts to prepare you for the full onslaught of THE WHOLE TRUTH.

It will be as if all the walls of your cosy homes as well as of your cosy, convenient and comfortable "belief systems"

ALL FALL DOWN AT ONCE,
LEAVING YOU ALONE, STRANDED, NAKED
AND PARALYSED IN DISBELIEF.

When you hear a strong wind, Beloveds, you may identify it as "stormy weather" which is disassociated with yourself and which you have to "put up with" for a while. According to its strength, it will prevent you from going about your usual routine. Many complain. But it would be more appropriate to ask WHERE IS IT COMING FROM or HOW WAS IT CREATED or WHAT WAS MY PART IN CREATING A STORM BY BLUSTERING FORWARD, or HOW DID I PROVOKE A STORM OR CONFLICT OR A DISAGREEMENT WHICH BURDENS THE ATMOSPHERE AND CHARGES IT NEGATIVELY?

The fact is that you are tied inextricably to the land, your earth. You are affected by her stormy emotions, by her struggles, by her pain, just as she is affected by your attempts to control her and exploit her resources. If there is too much suppression, and too much control, Earth will (LIKE YOU!) explode and say

NO: I AM NOT GOING TO DO THIS ANY MORE.

And so, she will break free, and you are destined to experience the consequences of that break. And so, like you when you feel persecuted and exhausted, she is bound to falter, to grind to a standstill and succumb to a long rest in order to recuperate. We are not saying pleasantries here or playing with metaphors.

SHE WILL SLOW DOWN AND STOP.
And all the exploitation and mishandling of Earth
will stop simultaneously.

Can you not hear her calling now, desperate for attention, desperate to warn you about the desperate measures she must take to feel comfortable, balanced and healed?

It is our duty to carry this message from Gaia to yourselves. It is a message of great love, for she sees and therefore understands EVERYTHING which is going on as you move and act on her skin. Her ability to discern is acute. Her knowledge of your habits and emotions is great, for she feels them all as if they were her own. AND THEY ARE, BECAUSE YOU ARE ALSO HER.

It is therefore with the deepest regret that she informs you
THAT SHE CANNOT CONTINUE IN THIS WAY.

SHE MUST TAKE ACTION TO
COUNTERACT THE ACCUMULATED NEGATIVITY.
IF SHE DOES NOT DO THIS,
IF SHE DOES NOT COME TO A COMPLETE STANDSTILL,

IT WILL BE THE END OF HER,
AND THUS IT WILL ALSO BE THE END OF YOU.

Know therefore of her great love for you all, and that her actions are a last effort to "save" those who are willing to see her as an intimate companion on their journey. Seraphin

EARTH SINGS: HEAR MY CRY

Please leave behind all our sorrow,
Try to see my tears when I cry
Please see tomorrow when you walk upon my skin
You will always, always, yes you will always be loved.

So wake up all my children, oh time to break illusion, see the lie
So wake up all my children, time to face confusion, asking why
So wake up every nation, stop the condemnation, see the lie
So wake up every country, time to form the cosmic family.

Please see the things you've forgotten,
Try to see the darkness in your past,
Please see the mirror when you look upon my soul
You will always, always, yes you will always be loved

Please don't remove all my treasures,
Try to clear the debris from my seas,
Please curb your battles when you live upon my soil
You will always, always, yes you will always be loved.

So wake up all my children, time to break illusion, see the lie
So wake up all my children, time to face confusion, asking why
So wake up every nation, stop the condemnation, see the lie
So wake up every country, time to form the cosmic family

So wake up all my children, oh see through the delusion
Hear my cry
So wake up all my children, we will stay together,
If only you can hear my cry

https://rjspirit100.bandcamp.com/track/hear-my-cry

Seraphin Message 555

GARDEN OF SOULS

Through Rosie, 5th March 2024

Do you think that you are here, Beloveds, to simply grow your physical bodies from the point of "fertilisation of the egg" to the point where you face a continual battle with aging, resulting ultimately and inevitably in "death"?

Is that the "meaning of life" for you?

The majority on your earth are actually concerned with their experience on a purely physical level, yet even those who are born into dire circumstances, where supporting the physical body is an overwhelming and constant struggle, are invited to discover that there is something more – that which we term "spiritual growth".

The words "soul", "spirit" and "spiritual" are used in various and often misleading ways in your various languages, and it is not possible for most of you to understand exactly what your "spirit" or "soul" might actually be.

We would present soul to you as THE ESSENTIAL PART OF YOURSELF WHICH IS INCORRUPTIBLE in the sense that it does not physically age and cannot be destroyed (unless you will it), in the same sense that it is the ESSENCE OF ALL LEARNING EXPERIENCES YOU HAVE UNDERGONE. It is the part of you which REMAINS WHEN PHYSICAL TRAPPINGS FAIL. In short, it is unaffected by what you refer to as death, which - for us - is simply going through a door into a new room.

Concerning "spirit", this has little to do with ghosts or negative entities (those these exist). This is the DIVINE LIFE FORCE WHICH IS TO BE FOUND IN EVERYTHING, whether it is "building" a soul essence or not. A stone, for example, is not developing a soul, but it contains "spirit" in the sense that is a part of the animate system which constitutes the body of the earth, herself a living entity with a soul, and filled with "spirit".

Earth, therefore, is a special garden where seeds – in effect YOURSELVES – are provided with the opportunity to grow, not only physically as a result of the gifts which nature generously presents to you, but also SOUL GROWTH in the form of various experiences and learning lessons which are ONLY TO BE FOUND HERE. And you have taken the decision to take all this on, even before incarnating, and after long discussion with various guides whose aim will always be YOUR SOUL GROWTH.

This is why, simply put, a humble fisherman in one life may incarnate as a queen in the next, or why a hermit in one life may choose to incarnate in a situation which encourages him to become a politician or public speaker in the next. In the end, you will have experienced ALL CONDITIONS, however beneficial and supportive, or however detrimental and crushing, to emerge as someone who is always anchored in serenity and who can DEAL WITH ANYTHING.

Many of you here have deliberately chosen one of the STEEPEST LEARNING CURVES THAT HAS EVER BEEN.

Those who can deal with everything will be in an excellent position to deal with what is to come. Whereas this will involve chaos and destruction on a physical level, the main challenge will be on a completely different level.

You will be required to do one mental "U-turn" after another, in an extensive and exhausting learning program

We observe your fear and hesitancy at the present time, for though you do not know what is nearly upon you, you sense that it will be monumental, and in this you are certainly correct. Yet it will also be a monumental step on the path of returning to the state of the "garden", and here we refer to those who came here a very long time ago to upgrade your DNA, thus allowing you to develop spiritually at a much higher pace.

That experiment long ago (which has mistakenly developed into the myth of Adam and Eve) failed to reach completion, yet this time, the job will be finished.

This is such a huge topic that we inevitably fail to do it justice here in these few short sentences, yet know that the celestial hierarchy is keeping the "Earth garden" under close observation and will provide clear instructions so that all "seeds" on earth will have optimal conditions to grow. Those which do not manage to germinate now, on the other hand, will be removed to different "soil" and to conditions more suitable to their slower pace of spiritual growth.

The world "momentous" again comes to mind as we see the "storm" approaching which will "kick start" these massive developments on all levels.

Travel well and remain
anchored in the knowledge
of your divinity.

Seraphin.

Seraphin Message 556

THE DIVINE PLAN INVOLVES YOU ALL

Through Rosie 7th March 2024

For the majority on Earth, this sentence will seem like some sort of esoteric nonsense, far from the "reality" of their daily lives. People will instantly reject it because the word DIVINE is rarely used, rarely contemplated, and even more rarely understood. Many would possibly relate it to religion of some sort, presuming that the sentence has been given any "second thought" at all.

We want to impress on you today that this has nothing to do with any established religion and that YES, THERE IS A PLAN which is presently invisible to the eyes of many, and YES, IT HAS TO DO WITH EACH OF YOU INDIVIDUALLY, AS WELL AS WITH YOUR FATE AS A COLLECTIVE.

It is not possible to "escape" or ignore the plan in its final unfolding. Although the plan has not yet revealed itself fully, there are hints scattered here and there for those who are somewhat "awake", who keep their eyes trained on the horizon, who are aware of any unusual happenings or movements. They may have been training themselves to do this for years, whereas others have concentrated solely on themselves and their immediate surroundings and companions, ignoring that there may be a further horizon at all.

You may ask: how can you, a humble and ordinary person who has perhaps not made any significant mark on the history of humanity as a whole, be considered a part of something divine. This is where you are in major error. It is precisely this sort of thinking which has led to the DEMISE OF THE DIVINE PLAN, and which has forced the celestial hierarchy to take radical (as yet unseen) steps to redeem it.

Thus you have been – due to your inattention, lethargy and stupidity – responsible for its incompletion.

IF YOU KNOW THIS, THEN IT MUST BE CLEAR TO YOU THAT YOU CAN ALSO REBUILD THAT PLAN WITH OUTSIDE HELP.

What is the DIVINE PLAN, you may ask?

IT IS A MAJOR STRATEGY ON MYRIAD LEVELS TO CLEANSE YOUR EARTH OF ALL NEGATIVE FREQUENCIES, CONFLICTS AND CONTAMINATION, AND TO REPLACE THOSE WITH HIGH FREQUENCY MATERIALS, EVENTS AND INTENTIONS WHICH WILL LEAD TO COMPLETE PEACE AND PROSPERITY ON EARTH FOR THE WHOLE OF HUMANITY.

Earth, in short, will become a HUMANE place to live, instead of the prison it presently constitutes. It is so difficult for us to believe THAT YOU HAVE NOT NOTICED YOUR ENSLAVEMENT, yet this is undoubtedly true.

We come to you today to reiterate HOW IMPORTANT YOUR EVERY THOUGHT AND ACTION IS FOR THE FUTURE OF YOUR WORLD.

This will become increasingly clear as you are presented with what you have actually produced as a result of your actions in the past – an unbearable and corrupted society.

Do we speak harshly?

No, we speak only the truth, and our effort here is to present it to you in a much gentler way than is expected in the future, when you will get it – to put not too fine a point upon it - "shoved brutally in your face". Our words are kind and gentle in comparison, and we speak to you out of love. Seraphin

Seraphin Message 557
CHANGING THE SHAPE OF YOUR LIVES

Through Rosie, 12th March 2024

Imagine, Beloveds, that you are square in shape, and imagine what it would feel like to become ROUND. You might see yourself, as this scribe did, with arms and legs stretched apart as in the drawing of Vitruvian Man by Leonardo da Vinci. If you take on this shape, you will suddenly be able to roll anywhere at lightning speed while rotating within this sphere. This is a metaphor for how quickly and how radically the changes will be upon you, providing you stretch out your arms to meet them.

On the other hand, you may choose to retreat instead, cowering in a corner, protected by immoveable walls as opposed to flexible round surfaces. If this is your choice, it must be clear to you that you will not travel, and thus will not progress. It is necessary to "move", leaving all your possessions and many of your beliefs behind you. It will be no good clamouring or holding onto your "roots" for dear life, and in this regard, we would draw your attention to the tumbleweed which will roll many miles across the desert in the strong wind. This plant is round. It is cut off from its roots and it carries its seeds with it to another terrain. This is another analogy of what stands before you.

The energy of a curve is a fascinating phenomenon, especially if a curved line – after some travelling – joins up to meet ITSELF, as in the ouroboros, the snake which bites its own tail to form a circle. Another example is the figure of eight which symbolizes harmony, balance and eternity.

And the "greatest" of those shapes in the CIRCLE. You may start in the middle, which is your DIVINE REFERENCE POINT* (we refer you to our previous message of this name) and then you may gradually spiral outwards, keeping the centre in view.

Thus you grow and transform, but you are still
ANCHORED BY THE SACRED CENTRE.
AND IT IS ESSENTIAL TO REMEMBER THIS NOW,
WHEN THE SHAPE OF YOUR LIVES
IS ABOUT TO CHANGE DRAMATICALLY.

Nobody can take this divine centre from you without your permission. This means that you can always retain stability and focus whatever happens., This means you can always refer back for help and guidance.

THIS MEANS THAT YOU ARE ALWAYS
CONNECTED TO THE DIVINE.

The other circular MOVING SHAPE we would like to draw your attention to is the TAURUS. Just as there is an electro-magnetic taurus pattern operating around your earth, with the appearance of a large doughnut endlessly turning itself inside out, YOU ARE SURROUNDED BY THE SAME SHAPE IN THAT YOUR THOUGHTS AND ENERGY STREAM UPWARDS AND FALL DOWN AGAIN ON ALL SIDES, LIKE A FOUNTAIN, ONLY TO RETURN TO YOURSELF IN AN NEVER-ENDING CYCLE.

The more advanced among you will be able to visualize this taurus around yourselves taking on the dimensions of the whole earth. Thus can you spread love everywhere, if you wish.

With this we hope again to impress upon you that what you send out returns to you eventually, in the same sense that being gentle to others automatically means the return of gentleness to oneself. The same is true of violence.

You will soon be entering an age in which ALL PREVIOUS SHAPES – especially pyramid schemes and power structures – will be brought under extreme scrutiny. Often they will be BROUGHT DOWN. Strict hierarchies which intended harm will be dissolved. Round tables will be used and round houses will be built. Ideas will be "passed around" and developed laterally rather than being imposed without question on an unsuspecting populace from "on high".

On the other hand, if new rules and regulations are imposed by your new celestial and very well-meaning "overlords", it is because they are preventing your extermination, and with time you will understand why such draconian measures are necessary.

KNOW THAT YOU WILL PLAY A GREAT PART ALSO
IN ESTABLISHING NEW RULES AND PARAMETERS.
Imagine that everything which burdens or obstructs your way
to fulfilling visions which benefit humanity JUST FALLS AWAY,
AND THAT YOU ARE FREE TO SUGGEST
AND JOINTLY DECIDE WHAT COMES NEXT.

We hope, through this text, to have whet your appetite for changing the shape of your present lives entirely, in order to increase global prosperity, abundance, peace and happiness. We remain watchful over your progress. Seraphin

*Seraphin Message 172

REMEMBERING THE REFERENCE POINT
IN CIRCLES OF GROWTH

Through Rosie, 17th February 2014

Imagine you are closing your eyes on a bright summer's day.
You can feel the glorious heat of the sun on your skin.
You are completely cocooned in warmth and light.
You are content and at peace, in tune with nature.

You are ONE with DIVINE CREATION.

You rest for a while, knowing bliss, knowing silence,
knowing the Source from which all motion springs.

You then reflect that to move away from this point of stillness
would make you appreciate it even more. It would take you away
from your REFERENCE POINT, would give you the experience
of DIFFERENCE, and you would develop a deep and meaningful
RELATIONSHIP to the reference point as opposed to being continually surrounded by its beauty and eternal repose and wisdom.

You reflect that to FORGET and then to REMEMBER the point
of reference would be a joyful journey, capable of inspiring others
on their journey, for whom the reference point is perhaps just a
naïve and pleasant but unreal dream.

And so you, like a tree trunk creating new layers,
pass through ever-increasing circles of your own making,
which take you further away from the reference point,
but which are compassed by the reference point,
as it remains at the very centre of ALL CIRCLES.

Your decision to step away temporarily from the reference point
of ALL CREATION is taken. You take the opportunity to enter the

physical, as a soul entering a physical body. Still are you sur-rounded by a protective shield of fluid warmth. Still are all your needs provided for. Still your eyes are closed.

You may perceive laughter, you may perceive tears, for both with rock you in your watery idyll inside the one you will call your "mother", but you are not yet initiated into the circle which starts outside the womb.

When you feel the regular pulsation around you growing ever stronger, as you are pushed out into the next circle of experience, you become heavy, separate, cold, helpless. You cry to attract attention. You laugh spontaneously. You love instantly. You still retain the memory of the ONE CREATION where LOVE is ALL AND EVERYWHERE.

Now you are sometimes left unsupported. You are no longer nourished instantly, but at regular intervals. You cannot move fast. You try, but then you must sleep to recover from exertion. Your determination is staggering. You will try again and again to stand. Your curiosity knows no bounds. You will turn your face to every stranger. You will believe everything you are told. You be-lieve in a happy and friendly world where nothing is to be feared.

You are devastated when, for reasons of lack, impatience or dan-ger – you are told NO. You are forced to re-assess, re-address, re-act, restrain and retract. Sometimes you repeat and some-times you retreat. You may choose to repeat one time, and then retreat. You may choose to repeat 100 times or you may choose to retreat without trying. You try to survive. You develop strate-gies to deal with the IMPERFECTIONS FACING YOU. You develop creativity, ingenuity and flexibility during this journey IF you look upon each situation anew, if you step into a BIGGER CIRCLE to experiment further.

In the next circle, you may experiment with friendship or loss, risk or complacency, goals or resignation, compliance or refusal to co-operate, love or jealousy, patience or impatience.

If you are not too busy, if you listen closely, you may hear the voice of peace and beauty calling from the other side of the wall, calling you into the next circle of experience.

You may decide to vacate your present circle or position
or activity or relationship for respite
in the hallowed walls of a sacred circle,
a sanctuary which reminds you
OF THE SOURCE FROM WHENCE YOU CAME.

Such a sojourn of "time-out" may strengthen you in your search, in your vocation, in your contribution to aligning your world with what you have REMEMBERED AS BEING IDEAL.

So where do you find yourselves at present, Beloveds? Can you move from one circle to the next with ease? Or do you move slowly with great regret, constantly looking behind you? Or do you move with grace and in anticipation of new and joyful experiences? Do you feel the glow of CREATION within you which lights and lightens each experience and which brightens all colours on your way?

Do you shout your truth or do you
DISPLAY it through your ACTIONS?

When you are pressed against a wall, do you return hurriedly to the old circle or do you seek a new one? Do you vacillate between extremes (I WILL EMANCIPATE MYSELF FULLY followed by THERE IS NOTHING I CAN DO)? Do you clean your mental windows? Do you close your mental shutters when the light is too bright, or when the truth is too much to bear? Do you close your mind to unpleasant facts? Can you bring back life to dormant desires? Can you recognise decay?

Are you observant? Do you see the clouds blown in one direction, and then in another? Know that you can decide whether to stay or go, whether to lead or follow, whether to act upon repeated signs of warning or whether to carry on as usual. You may learn to discern or you may continue to judge everything at face value. Do you see the unseen as well as the seen?

Do you see what is hidden as well as what is disclosed? Are you aware that your limitations, as you perceive them, can always be broken?

Are you moving forward or do you automatically retreat in self-protection? You may question or continue to accept. You may stagnate or you may grow. ALL IS CHOICE. You may live or you may die, for this is what "death" is – the decision to terminate GROWTH on the spiritual plane, which is reflected in the demise of the body on the physical plane.

And when you reach this, your final circle, are you passive and resigned and without hope, or are you still racing around with horns blasting in search of the ultimate external excitement, at-tempting to distract yourselves from the fear of not knowing what lies behind the final wall, or have you learnt to look back reflec-tively, gathering up your experience and gift it to others? Are you still struggling or are you secure in your knowledge that you are returning to your Source?

And so your circles develop. They are endless, until you decide – consciously or subconsciously – that the lesson is learnt and that your experience of separation is complete. Then will you step again into the golden yellow light of DIVINE CREATION, back to the reference point from whence you came.

Seraphin Message 558
THE PREGNANT PAUSE

Through Rosie 17th March 2024

For those who have ever been pregnant and who have delivered a child, thus changing your lives forever, the present dominant feeling of tension may feel somehow familiar (it includes some trepidation and joy, despite having no real idea about who and what is going to grace your lives with their sudden presence).

However, we can assuredly say that
NOTHING CAN PREPARE YOU FOR WHAT IS COMING.

You may think that you have taken precautions for every possible eventuality, but these precautions are suited to scenarios which your limited imagination produces.

THE TRICK IS TO EXPAND YOUR IMAGINATION
AND ADMIT MUCH GREATER POTENTIAL SCENARIOS
INTO YOUR CONSIDERATION,
SO THAT YOU MAY FARE BETTER,
OR SO THAT YOU ARE EVEN SAILING
ON THE CREST OF A WAVE IN HIGH ELATION.

Thus you can see that the best preparation is not only physical, though that will also play an important part, but mental and spiritual. We would like to see your "spirit" – the DIVINE PART OF YOURSELF, soar like a bird on the horizon as dawn breaks, as it will, after a very long period of darkness. Ideally, you will now be "pregnant" with a whole plethora of wonderful ideas which are begging "birth", to be implemented when the "light of day" finally arrives.

Ideally, you will USE THE DARKNESS to experiment with everything which produces "light" and which raises the vibration.

As always, it is your CHOICE – whether to attempt to raise the vibration of your neighbour, of a friend, of a stranger, of a piece of land, of a busy place or of your home, or whether you CHOOSE to leave them at the same low level of vibration you found them in. YOUR RADIANCE AND YOUR ACTIONS WILL MAKE A DIFFERENCE

This piece is entitled THE PREGNANT PAUSE, not because there is any pause in pregnancy (a new world will inevitably be born when the time is right) but because there will be a mental pause during the pregnancy.

THIS WORLDWIDE PAUSE WILL FAST-TRACK
THE GERMINATION OF NEW IDEAS,
NEW PROJECTS AND NEW WAYS OF BEHAVIOUR,
ALL BASED ON NEW PRINCIPLES.

This pause, which will reduce all outward distractions, which will interrupt all automatic reactions, which will disconnect you from all crutches and which will offer you RECONNECTION TO YOUR GODLY SELF, will affect everyone worldwide, and it will give everyone the chance to reflect on their lives and to examine whether they fit in with the new parameters and stipulations which will unapologetically be GODLY ONES, AND WHICH HAVE BEEN REJECTED AND IGNORED FOR MILLENNIA. It is our greatest wish that you are able to use this "pause" to develop your visions for the future and that you use it also to assist and guide those who have never been forced to stop in their tracks, with the result that there was not adequate time for self-reflection or true recovery, let alone to be stopped and confronted with a "pause" of such formidable dimensions, and pregnant with SUCH POTENTIAL. We are surveying your actions closely and we send you our love and support in these most difficult of times, Seraphin.

Seraphin Message 559

STEPPING BACK TO MOVE FORWARD
or OH MY GOD

Through Rosie, 23rd 2024

Can you imagine, Beloveds, that we are capable of monitoring how often you say OH MY GOD? This is the phrase to which the majority resort when they are suddenly confronted with great tragedy, or, alternatively, with great joy. In either case, you cannot believe what is unravelling before your very eyes, often without any sort of warning.

Exclamations of OH MY GOD are collectively on the increase, and this will turn into a cumulative curve which sky rockets upwards as atrocities increase and as counteractive measures taken by the "good guys" / "white hats" / REPRESENTATIVES OF GOD similarly increase.

You can be sure that all your small hang-ups, supposed problems and minor irritations will then appear to you as bagatelles without any import or meaning. We are again trying to prepare you for what is to come, which we are not allowed to reveal, but we are permitted to reveal the VASTNESS and ENORMOUS CONSEQUENCES of actions to come, both ungodly and godly.

In one way, the "ungodly" is allowed to play out, rather than being nipped in the bud, SO THAT IT CAN BECOME VISIBLE TO ALL. It is only following this visibility that it will be fully understood by all. Then it will be clear that godly countermeasures are fully justified and fully necessary. This is what we mean by the necessity to take a step back, allowing tragedies to unfold, allowing secrets to surface and allowing evil to raise its terrible head, in order to move forward AS ONE with full understanding of the fact that the termination of evil is completely necessary and THE ONLY WAY.

You can be sure that the celestial hierarchy has considered all options and that it will always choose an option which will "wake up" the most people, thus providing an opportunity to further spiritual maturity. The hierarchy will always choose an option which TAKES AS MANY SOULS WITH IT AS POSSIBLE.

This suggests that some people will be lost, as it sadly the case. Many will feel helpless and will not understand. Others will refuse to recognize the evil, and some are indeed part of it.

Their stubborn stance will earn a harsh response.

Before we depart, we would again like to comment on your favourite expression OH MY GOD which is used so copiously, whether the individual is of religious persuasion or not.

We smile somewhat sadly when we see you fall into a lower frequency with these words, for it is a call of despair, hoping that a greater power will intervene. Intervene we will, but only at the appointed time when that which is godly can be accepted.

The contradiction within this phrase is that

YOU ARE CALLING UPON YOURSELF,
FOR YOU ARE GOD,
AND INDEED ACTIVATION OF YOUR GODLINESS
IS THE ANSWER TO ALL ILLS.

Thus we leave you on the eve of great new developments.

Seraphin.

Seraphin Message 560

A HOLE IN ONE: CELESTIAL POWER

Through Rosie, 30th and 31st March 2024,
at the break of Easter Day

Dearest Inhabitants on Earth: it is time to give you a brief insight into our actions as part of the celestial administration which is responsible for this universe. And yes, there are many universes.

The majority of you, if you were to entertain the idea at all, would be very surprised to discover that your governments, international organisations and judicial systems are not the highest "entities". They are not the ultimate authority, and they certainly do not act in unity and with integrity, which is actually the hallmark of universe administration.

EARTH IS SUBJECT TO UNIVERSE GOVERNMENT,
WHICH RULES IN ORDER TO SERVE ALL CITIZENS
SO THAT THEY CAN REALISE THEIR BEST ENDEAVOURS
IN SERVICE TO THE ONE.

Is this what you hear your own governments proclaim?
Have they even managed to secure global peace?

The answer is NO, and this means that they are
NOT IN ALIGNMENT WITH COSMIC LAW,
AND NEITHER DO THEY RECOGNISE THOSE (in effect US)
WHOSE TASK IT IS TO ENSURE
THAT THESE LAWS ARE KEPT,
FOR THEY LEAD TO
UNIVERSAL PEACE, PROSPERITY AND ABUNDANCE.

Surely this is what you would like to see.

We would like to remind you of the following:

ALL THIS IS POSSIBLE IF YOUR GLOBAL GOVERNMENTS SURRENDER TO US. AND YES, IT IS A WAR IN THE SENSE THAT YOUR "CIRCUS DIRECTORS" ARE AT COMPLETE ODDS WITH OUR HIGH STANDARDS AND EXTREMELY NOBLE INTENTIONS. And we would like to mention that your corrupt governments would not be able to wield such despotic power IF YOU THE PEOPLE DID NOT ALLOW IT.

We now come to our title: A HOLE IN ONE. Celestial administration has been in existence for much longer than you can imagine. It has seen this earth develop, from the very early stages, moving through great cataclysm and various different ages, populated by diverse peoples, and colonized by various cosmic visitors. There have been dark ages and golden ages. There have been great wars (yes, ones you have never heard about) and great times of peace. There have been rebellions and secret counter rebellions which still exist today. And this is so much more complicated and so much more expansive than the stories contained in your faulty, manipulative and incomplete history books.

In brief, the members of the universe administration have seen so much, have had so much experience and have been so active on many unseen levels that it is impossible to make a faulty move. It is as if ageless beings of ultimate serenity and wisdom are at the helm, which is indeed the case.

Even if they make a decision leading to tragedy, such as sending a messenger into a "den of lions" (in your designation, the sending of Jesus to your Middle East) they will do so IN FULL AWARENESS THAT THE "TRAGEDY" WILL EVENTUALLY TURN INTO VICTORY, and this is the point where you find yourselves at the moment. The potential and effect of such a messenger cannot be underestimated, and there will be a moment when everything will be understood. THE PENNY WILL DROP.

So, because we have so much insight, wisdom and power to think ahead, considering all eventualities, we can never go wrong (and we see some of you shaking your heads in disbelief, because you can very clearly see all that is going wrong so dreadfully in your world at present).

But once our decision is made, all else will fall into the background and we will aim immediately and unerringly for our goal, just like an excellent golfer who – irrespective of weather, irrespective of terrain, irrespective of his own emotions and irrespective of the cataclysmic events around him - is always capable of getting a HOLE IN ONE.

This is our announcement that we will move swiftly and with great accuracy once the decision is taken to strike the blow, irrespective of all else.

This "blow" will hit deep into your minds,
causing you to question nearly all facets of your lives.

Are you ready for this?

We suspect not, for it has not been your training to expect "galactic outsiders" to enter into your reality, but we say to you that this is inevitable.

This scribe is very tired, as it is just after midnight and the dawn of your Easter, so we will end here.

Know that we will arrive and know that this will be the beginning of something completely new which will throw all of your history and past life into relief, making it appear as a rather unpleasant and distant dream.

Seraphin

Seraphin Message 561

THE OPEN DOOR

Through Rosie, 7th April 2024

Many of you on Earth continue to live your lives in complete res-ignation and sadness, convinced that nothing will ever change for the better, trying sometimes to warn others about the steadily deteriorating morals and encroachments on peaceful activities, including all those which give rise to great joy. They are in an extremely pessimistic frame of mind right now.

Others, such as you reading this message, will have a glimmer-ing of hope because you glimpsed a GREATER PERSPECTIVE, and in fact anyone can do this – irrespective of their circum-stances and location – by surveying the sky on a clear night.

You may even conclude, as this scribe did recently, that there are more "stars" than usual, and that they are brighter. We would say that it is time to let your imaginations roll and to look hopefully to the heavens.

Some of you have referenced "portals" and "wormholes", and these are supposedly DOORS TO OTHER WORLDS. While these ideas and conjurings of your imaginations are actually in their infancy in this respect, there are indeed "doors open" to those who realise that they are presently living in a prison ward.

Again, we repeat, it is of your own collective making and it covers millennia. You.may ask yourselves what you have to do with this long period of time in view of your short lifespan, but we remind you that souls incarnate many times on this planet, mostly because they are not allowed off it until they reach a higher level of spirituality.

What we would like to say next is that THE DOOR IS ALWAYS OPEN, and that it is available by expanding both your hearts (for compassion and non-violence are essential and a prerequisite for moving forward) and your CURIOSITY. For even with compassion, without curiosity you would not start walking towards the door, even if you saw it, even if it were open.

Would you be curious enough to enter the door of a space craft, Beloveds? We would like to insinuate that you will have this experience in the future. There will be people who refuse to see this open door. There will be others who are too afraid to try it. There will be others who are incapable of leaving everything behind. We urge you to scrutinise your situations (violent, corrupt, unsafe, depressed) and ask yourselves whether you can actually leave them behind, or whether you are too ensconced in the "familiar" yet sub-optimal. Huge choices are about to be faced by you, inhabitants of earth. We remind you that there will be new doors open to you, and we urge you to enter. We are looking down of what will be a great transition for your planet. Seraphin

Seraphin Message 562
THE HEART OF THE MATTER
AND THE TASK OF THE MIND

Through Rosie, 16th April 2024

Dear Inhabitants of Earth: those who have done some sort of work on themselves, which involves considerable self-reflection and reframing, including seeing everything you see as a reflection of yourself, will be tested to a slightly lesser degree in the incoming chaos because they will be able to centre themselves and because they will be able to see everything from a more distant and philosophical point of view.

It is all the more difficult to hold your ground in difficult circumstances, and this is what so many of our CHOSEN ONES (which is YOU READING THIS) are going through right now, faced with opposition" of all kinds. It has often been said that the "winds of change" are best weathered by becoming like a blade of grass which bends before the wind. While this is a useful metaphor for staying centred, the coming situation also requires action on a level you have not previously experienced.

In many case you will be witnessing people who cannot cope and who are in extreme emotional distress, and it will be your challenge to respond FROM THE HEART and to find it in yourself to help those whom you may have previously despised or ridiculed or looked down upon for their choices so far. But this should not be your focus. While positive criticism has its place, it should not override compassion.

The "heart of the matter" is indeed THE HEART.

And it is because the heart has been neglected as a parameter in so many actions (war and destruction to mention the worst) that the situation is escalating before your very eyes.

Where is your sympathy for your "fellow man"
and "fellow women", beloveds?

And if you proclaim you are not fighting against "civilians", then who are you fighting against? All people are also civilians, in fact, it is impossible to separate this for example into the civilians and the government, or the civilians and the army, for they are intertwined and all affect each other, sometimes also supporting each other. To say you are not affecting civilians by sending off missiles to "strategic points" is very naive, because that negative energy will spread, because military who are killed have families, because industrial centres and their personnel provide for families, etc. etc.

So, what is the task of the mind, if the heart is so important? The heart can easily be manipulated by "dark forces", and so it requires protection in the form of critical appraisal and rational assessment. You may think that this is something we have often repeated, yet we cannot stress enough the ACUTE NATURE OF YOUR TIMES AND THE VERY REAL CHALLENGES YOU WILL BE FACING. This is merely a reminder of what your focus should be on, and how you can best some out of all this smiling. For us, this is so obvious, but watching you inhabitants of earth and how you conduct your relationships and your lives, it looks like most of you have actually LOST YOUR MINDS.

We salute all those who are presently taking up the "spiritual sword" and who are forming part of the "spiritual army" as opposed to the military factions which presently still dominate your earth, but which are destined to fall. Seraphin.

Seraphin Message 563:
LIVING A SHADOW OF EXISTENCE
AND MANIFESTING THE GOLDEN BALL

Through Rosie, April 2024

You may ask what is meant by "living a shadow of existence", Beloveds. This means that the life you are presently experiencing is just a shadow of what it could be, or of what it is - or has been - on other planets.

You can be sure that if you are going full pelt along one path, willing and enthusiastic about experiencing the fullness of life, with all its depths of joys and sorrows, having consolidating what is the best direction to take in order to make this a better and more perfect world, then do not be surprised that you will be stopped, because "full" and powerful emotions of this sort lead to radical action which threatens the "powers that be". It is not possible to move into this sort of existence because the opposition is so strong.

Having said that, it is getting weaker by the day, and so,
while you look upon the beautiful nuggets of nature on your
planet earth where fauna, animals and humans are living
in complete harmony with each other,
and which have a paradisical feel to them,
know that this is your future,
and know that what you are presently experiencing
is a cheap and shabby replica of

THE REAL.

Let this be of some sustenance to you during these dark and dull days where you may know that you are on the threshold of something new, but where this has not yet truly appeared in your "reality", thus you are somewhat "down in the dumps". We ask you to keep your eyes looking ever upwards, for the light will come, thus heralding this step into new possibilities and certainly into new paradises which cannot compare with the mundane, numbed, humdrum lives which you stumble through today.

We send you this message and surround you with our love, and we are here to tell you that you are so much more than this, and that if at present there are obstacles in your way, you are surely on the right path. For everything will be done to stop you, demoralize you, to sadden you, to corrupt you, and to make you stop. So, we ask you to continue walking in faith and to undertake the following "Golden Ball" exercise, and we will meet you when you come to the end of this path. Seraphin.

GOLDEN BALL EXERCISE

The intention of this exercise is to nurture the earth, sending her love and gratitude. She needs this energy at this time.

Imagine you are on the top of a very high mountain. Draw golden light down from the Central Universe / SOURCE OF ALL THAT IS and let it enter your crown chakra on each inhale. On each exhale, spread this golden light outside of yourself, first in your immediate surroundings, and then in an ever widening spiral until it reaches the horizon 360 degrees around you.

Continue this so that a layer of gold eventually covers the whole globe.

When the globe is covered, pour the golden light into the earth herself through a hole on the opposite side of the globe to yourself, until the golden ball becomes solid.

Seraphin Message 564

THE PARALYSIS OF ATTACHMENT

Through Rosie, 18th May 2024

Beloved inhabitants of earth who are so attached to various things, scenarios, circumstances, concepts, traditions and peo-ple. We would like to draw your attention to the very detrimental and destructive nature of such behavior. Note that we are talking about ATTACHMENT, not about LOVE, because the real concept of true love has as its core LETTING GO, which is the complete opposite of attachment.

Your worlds are full, your minds are crammed with thoughts constantly, trying to fit in as much as possible, trying to "live it up", trying to ensure that you don't miss out, trying to "hold on" to anything and everyone which passes your way.

This behavior is underlined by FEAR: fear that one day you will stand alone: fear that one day you will not have any possessions: fear that one day you will have no religion or comforting thoughts which prevent you falling into DESPAIR.

In the not too distant future you will be faced with a scenario which will force "dis-attachment" for most everyone. Those who are not used to living "in the flow" and who are not used to moving forward from one learning experience to another with ease, will find this very difficult. It will be as if they have fallen into a deep and bottomless pit, and as if they expect a very hard landing.

For some the landing will indeed be hard. Others, on the other hand, may enjoy the ride and fall "on their feet". Being stiff, almost "fossilised" in one's ideas and habits, will make the landing harder, for they are brittle, insubstantial and break easily.

Faith, on the other hand, can withstand all this.

At this stage you may ask FAITH IN WHAT?

And we would answer:

Faith in the fact (and it is a fact) that
your lives are guided with a view to
EXTENDING YOUR PERSPECTIVES, with regard to
INCREASING YOUR SPIRITUALITY, with regard to
INCREASING YOUR CAPACITY TO ASSIST OTHERS
and ultimately with regard to
INCREASING YOUR JOY.

If you can remember this, as you are falling full throttle into the "hole", you will be very well served.

So, will you be in this state of faith,
or will you fall into fear and thus into
PARALYSIS?

We can assure you that the latter will be of absolutely no use to the building up of a new family, a new community, a new nation and in fact a new league of nations under one command, as will be the case.

There will be no more clashing of opinions or searches for transparency. All will be clear. All will be humbled, and will be generally of the same accord, and so there will be no problem uniting under one "roof", which, we add, will be a beneficial and galactic roof, and not the New World Order which you have been suspecting. They will be defeated.

We have asked you before to imagine how it would be to suddenly have to leave all possessions, all fond imaginings, all static religious convictions and all political allegiances behind.

We remind you again that this is on the cards and rapidly approaching so that it OVERTAKES YOUR REALITY, rather than staying in the realm of the "news" which you may at times see on your phones or televisions.

It will hit you IN THE REAL, and it is – as always – our motivation to prepare you for this so that you are better equipped to pave the way for others and hold their hands during the coming "crossing over" into another world.

Love Seraphin.

Seraphin Message 565

THROUGH THE GATE OF PAIN
TO THE PATH OF PARADISE

Through Rosie, May 2024

For some, the gate of pain will remain forever closed, despite the enticing perspectives and possibilities which pave the journey beyond the gate. The view beyond the gate is enticing, yet the desire to remain in the shadows, keeping their range of emotions to a minimum, is preferable. They would rather remain "safe" and within familiar territory – even if they are imprisoned – than progressing to the next level which is true freedom.

It has often been said THE TRUTH WILL SET YOU FREE.

For it is this, Beloveds - moving through the pain - which will bring you to the greatest heights. This may seem like a contradiction, since a decision to take the plunge, question everything, experience everything, find your own personal quest and STICK WITH IT, which will involve a lot of struggle in the present environment. Yet the things you learn on the way and the encounters which enrichen you, and the experiences which are so wondrous that you will never forget them, even in your darkest hour, will actually bring you to a completely new level. You will have reached "higher ground", in fact, where the dense tornados of emotional turmoil can no longer reach you. It is thus worth entering the fray in order to distance yourselves from the chaos and confusion and to gain complete serenity.

Complete serenity is what will be required from you in the future, for although you may already have passed through the gate, there will be so many who are only now stepping out timidly on the same journey, and their turmoil will affect you, if you let it.

However, you can act as a beacon of inspiration, for you will already have managed to make it to the other side, sitting radiantly and confidently, guiding others as a DIVINE LIGHT.

What is this pain of which we speak, you may ask. It is as if you are in a very long relationship, into which you have put great effort and made much investment, and which you have never questioned until one day, you fall into suspicion and ask your partner

DO YOU REALLY LOVE ME?

From their delayed reaction and guilty look, you might immediately realise that love died long ago, without either of you really noticing it. Now you have to face it full on, and of course this is a very PAINFUL situation, all of which could have been avoided if you had not asked the question. Yet it will move both to "higher ground", increasing honesty and authenticity.

This is not an advocation to question marriage or longstanding relationships: it is merely a metaphor for the SEVERITY of the changes which will fall upon you once you start asking the right questions, for example:

ARE THERE ANY HONEST POLITICIANS? Or
WHY ARE THERE ONLY TWO POLITICAL PARTIES? Or
DO WE NEED POLITICAL PARTIES AT ALL? Or
WHY CAN'T OUR LEADERS SIMPLY BE RIGHTEOUS
AND RESPECTFUL HUMAN BEINGS
WHO ACT IN THE FAVOUR OF THE PEOPLE?

You can apply this sort of questioning to any areas of your lives, and in the end, you will pare down everything to the "nitty-gritty", by which we mean the MOST ESSENTIAL, THE MOST MORAL, THE MOST HONEST, THE MOST BENEFICIAL and ultimately THE MOST JOYFUL.

So think of us when you are given the key to the gate of pain. Will you take it and enter, feeling pain but also feeling vibrantly alive, or will you retire with haste and continue to live your limited lives, unconscious of what is really going on around you until it suddenly hits you in the face with a blow which is fatal.

We warn you today, like all days, that there is much that you will have to deal with, and we advise that you start with this sooner rather than later. This we advise in love, Seraphin

Seraphin Message 566:

FROM POISON TO PURITY: WHERE THE SACRED LIES

Through Rosie, 14th June 2024

Where does the sacred lie, Beloveds?

We assume – from our observance of behavior on your planet – that this is a question which you have rarely posed or seriously considered, distracted as you are by "worldly things", distracted as you are by the scramble to survive, distracted as you are by the mindless "entertainment" which sucks up all your "leisure time", specifically designed by your present controllers to keep you "busy" and pacified.

We would like to focus on the adjective "mindless", for such entertainment does all the thinking for you. You do not need to do anything except press a switch or click on a link. There is no creative effort on your part, and no pre-knowledge of what you will be presented with (the suspense is "killing" you). Similarly, you have no knowledge of the sublimal messages it is actually sending to your subconscious. Suffice to say that such entertainment in all arenas (including the political arena) encourages the very opposite of fearless, honest and determined action.

You are glued to the screen, and whatever it is showing you exerts 100% of your attention and complete fascination, putting you through an emotional washing machine. But they are not your emotions: they are merely "borrowed" and unreal. When you are in such a state of oblivion, you will not notice – unless perhaps you are a mother who is highly attuned to the cries of her child – the cries of the needy of desperate in your vicinity.

Is it not time, Beloveds, to disperse with the superficial
and seek the SACRED?

This is so easy: you can see it everywhere: in the perfect coordination of your hand movements (and here we refer to the hands of this scribe, writing down this message as we speak): in the eyes of everyone you meet, for everyone has a story to tell and a message to give which assists you to become WISER, MORE COMPASSIONATE, MORE AWARE, MORE ABLE TO LEARN, AND THUS MORE SACRED.

ATTEMPTING TO REACH THESE HEIGHTS OF PURITY,
PERFECT INTEGRITY, MEASURED REACTIONS
AND ABSOLUTE SERENITY IS YOUR GOAL.
AND IT IS YOUR GOAL ALSO TO SERVE AS
A TEMPLATE FOR OTHERS TO FOLLOW.

Thus it is YOUR DUTY ALSO to point out
THAT WHICH IS NOT SACRED,
FOR IT HAMPERS EVERYONE ON THE PATH DIVINE.

This may sound very strict and absolute to you, and indeed it is, necessarily so, for in the end (AND THAT DRAWS NEAR!) no deviations from the DIVINE will be tolerated. However radical this sounds, we ask you to comply.

You have but to contemplate the world around you: the nations massacred, the starving millions, the unprecedented levels of corruption, the dishonesty on all echelons, the global human trafficking networks, and the callous masters at the helm. You are being given one very hard and difficult "last look" at all these areas of abuse, and at all this POISON of which your earth must be purged.

You should be aiming for ABSOLUTELY PURITY OF MIND,
which will inevitably lead to behavior motivated by
good intentions and by compassion
and which also immediately pinpoints
ALL THAT WHICH IS NOT SACRED,
singling it out for immediate extermination.

Only thus can you live in eternal peace. Seraphin

Seraphin Message 567
THE LAST SAFARI

Through Rosie 14th June 2024

The time has come, Beloveds, for your last "safari", which means that you have a final chance to REVISIT THE PAST, assessing what was of value, what was destructive, where you sowed seeds, and what became of them (whereby we would stress that not all "good seeds" have been able to germinate due to very adverse conditions).

In short, where have you left your footprint, and did it have a positive effect? This is the yardstick which you are asked to use in your assessment. And if we widen this concept to "a good effect on others", then you may be catching on to what is of real importance here.

As more and more "landmarks" come into view, rising after being submerged from a dark and raging sea which is now retreating, you will automatically be taken on the journey of seeing your own personal landmarks in a new light, and unfortunately, this will not always be a joyful experience.

If you travel on a safari, you cross unknown land, always on the lookout for wildlife. You may experience sudden joy – the sight of a thousand flamingos by a lake – or you may experience great fear through the attack of a pride of lions.

As you pass through similar situations and emotions,
remember your DIVINE PROTECTION
and remember that the whole point of this exercise is to learn.

When the "safari" ends, you will find yourselves back home in familiar and "normal" surroundings, yet the knowledge gained during the safari will have changed your view of everything forever. We wish you good travels and a safe homecoming.

Seraphin

Seraphin Message 568
THE EAGLE HAS LANDED: MISSION POSSIBLE

Through Rosie, 2nd July 2024

When you hear or read the word "mission", this may well be associated in your minds with the word "impossible", yet we assure you that not only are you on a mission, but you are also on a mission which BREAKS ALL THE BOUNDARIES OF YOUR PRESENT COMPREHENSION and which – once you set of with dedication, determination and trust in that specific direction - IS MORE THAN POSSIBLE.

You have for the most part received educations which have impressed upon you your lack of knowledge (hence the pressure to gain knowledge). We would also like to emphasise the word "received", for you have remained mostly in a passive stance (unless your teachers have been truly exceptional and revolutionary and have conduced you into thinking, reflecting and creating content yourself, pushing you to recognize that the source of truth is WITHIN YOURSELF, only waiting to be consulted).

The fact that your active participation and independence has not been encouraged has led to the tendency to "receive" - without question - anything which comes along, including propaganda and false information. Yet no delay is in vain, and no detour can put you off the track permanently if you are open to learning from your experiences and if you frequently contact your inner voice.

You will soon learn that you and many other inhabitants on this planet have taken an ENORMOUS DETOUR from your original mission. The proof of this is that your mission is largely not clear to you, and you have not actively searched for that what is truth, or for that which elates you, or for that which simultaneously gives your life and the lives of others more meaning and quality.

To cower in a chair and kowtow to superiors without asserting your own opinion or offering contributions to the development of the process, the firm or the organization, is to remain firmly centred in the role of polite but ineffective "employee". Some of you will discover that you have played this role to the hilt, neglecting your skills and potential.

YOU ARE NOT RETIRING WALLFLOWERS
BUT CREATURES OF DIVINE POTENTIAL.

A number of you who read this will be aware of the vastness of their mission, of the fact that they are an essential cog in a mass movement to free and better your earth. Your importance, and also the knowledge of your importance, cannot be underestimated at this crucial time when so many things are in the balance, AND IT IS UP TO EACH ONE OF YOU TO DETERMINE WHICH WAY THE SCALES WILL TIP.

We would like to thank all those who have held out so far, despite all odds, despite multiple incarnations throughout many prior civilisations – all of which have managed to destroy themselves due to lack of spiritual development. But this time, you will see the results of your efforts, and after a temporary "collapse", you will be in an excellent position to excel, to flourish, and ultimately to enjoy and also to provide "happiness" and qualities much lacking on the planet at the moment due to all sorts of oppression.

As for our mission, which is to guide you on yours, we would say that THE EAGLE HAS LANDED and that this particular mission of ours is drawing to a close, though we will attend you to the end. We wish you strong nerves and great presence of mind during this final stage. Seraphin.

Seraphin Message 569

THE HOT AIR BALLOON

Through Rosie, 12th July 2024

Dear Inhabitants on Earth: you are all in for a "hot air balloon" experience, by which we mean that you are to rise slowly and silently, leaving your immediate and familiar surroundings behind to climb to a completely different level, from which you will survey the surface from an entirely different view.

You will see the "patterns" created by all movement. You might be able to see the cars and people moving around on the ground. You may not always know or see what they are doing individually.

You may not know their specific aim (at least not while you are still in the air), but you will recognize where they are going and what they are creating COLLECTIVELY, and it is this aspect which is of paramount importance, since the conditions on your planet are not primarily the result of individual policies but of COLLECTIVE BEHAVIOUR.

Similarly, you will see "patterns of power" – how the "shakers and movers" with power at their fingertips have coerced the movements of the rest. If you are observant, you will also see how these power centres are presently crumbling.

From your position on high, you will be able to perceive the pitfalls into which so many have fallen, as well as the mountain summits which have been climbed. The past – as well as the possible future – will be mapped out before you in a way you never thought possible, and with a clarity unprecedented, including "patterns" never before perceived or recognized by those on the ground, and though you may have suspected some of these, you will still not have conceived of the depths or heights to which this civilisation (and previous civilisations) have risen and fallen.

There are of course those who will never "take off", who will never step into the hot air balloon to go on this voyage of discovery. Typically, they will feel threatened by anything which is radically different or which challenges their world view. They prefer to remain "grounded" and limited in knowledge, never daring to imagine there may be so much more to their lives, and never realizing that they have so much potential.

Then again there will be those who board but who will be "blinded" by the clarity of what is shown to them. Even at this stage, they may shield their eyes and beg to descend …

The opposite of descending is ascending: "ascension" is a word which has been used vastly and misleadingly on your world to suggest a state of enlightenment which is suddenly reached.

We would like to reiterate that
YOU WILL WORK TOWARDS YOUR OWN "ASCENSION",
and that there is nothing sudden about it:

It is a continuous process - not something you "move into". It is – roughly speaking – the point at which the spiritual aspect of your life surmounts the physical and material aspects, when you apply wisdom gained in your daily life, when you are in alignment with cosmic law rather than dictated by personal desires.

And this spiritual growth is NOT A STATIC STATE:
you cannot "reach enlightenment"
and then sit on your laurels.

The very nature of a spiritual life is that spirituality always increases and that you are continuously on a learning journey.

Thus can your journey in the "hot air balloon" be part of an astonishing learning process, and one which is necessary to preserve your earth. For on high you will see her wounds, the blemishes on her skin, the areas of devastation, death and destruction.

All this will you feel personally,
and thus will you know that your personal choices
either benefit or destroy her.

We wish you good travels and a piercing eye to determine the "lay of the land", discovering what is your next optimal move.
We support you during these perilous times.

Seraphin.

Seraphin Message 570
YOUR LIFE: AN ARTWORK OR A CESSPIT?

Through Rosie, 31st July 2024

Dear inhabitants of Earth: you are rapidly moving towards a new point of "departure" and a new crisis point which will require momentous decisions on your part. It will involve – in the light of new information and circumstances – the reframing of your life so far. That is to say, that if you have a certain picture of yourself or if you are convinced of your own identity or status in the world, you will be forced to think again in a very radical way.

We would like to ask you this:
if your life were a painting, what would it look like?

All artists – and you are one of them in the sense that you are the creator of your own life's events, and you the one who chooses how to react to events which seemingly originate outside of your-selves (we say "seemingly" because it is not quite that simple, and you indeed do carry some responsibility) – to repeat, all art-ists have different ways of approaching the canvas – the pure white unsullied canvas which is the state of your "life" at birth.

One artist may choose a very fine brush, painting very delicate colours in one corner, leaving the majority of available space empty. Others may fall into the ecstasy of creation, ripping huge tubes of paint open with their teeth and squirting them randomly on the canvas. Yet others may solemnly take the biggest brush and methodically paint the whole canvas black. Yet others may say a prayer before starting and dedicate their work – which is often work on themselves – to the better understanding and ben-efit of others. Some wish to throw their emotions onto the canvas. Some wish to please their audience. Others could not care less what anyone else thinks of their work. Some are intensely aware of the effect that every stroke of the brush will have on the viewer.

Know that all these paintings of your lives, which reflect all your choices and creations during life, are going to be put on show in an enormous art gallery. They will be seen and reviewed by celestial judges. They will be assessed for their meaning, beauty, beneficial effect and legacy. They will be sorted into those which inspire and those which depress. They will be scrutinized for potential, for signs of openness to change, for proof of a benevolent attitude towards others.

They will be checked to see if there is any "divine spark" which has manifested itself in the colours or themes.

Do you think we are going too far with this analogy, Beloveds? Believe, me, we are only just getting started.

Again, we ask you to imagine what the "picture of your life" would look like, for indeed you have painted it so, and indeed it does exist in the annals of the cosmic records for others to see. And when you have imagined this picture, imagine that this canvas is placed on another canvas which is 1000 times bigger.

This "reframing" is about to happen.
This is not to make you feel small.
It is designed to make you feel your potential.

This is an attempt to warn you about what is yet to come, as well as the long road in front of you, which we may refer to as "the eternal journey". Yet this is only possible if there is some merit in the painting of your present lives.

If, on the other hand, no such merit can be found, anything which is remotely positive on the canvas (in the sense that we have already mentioned) will be cut out from the rest and placed on a new canvas. This is, in effect, what you have learnt in this life, and what you will retain during your next one.

If no such positive element can be found,
and if your painting resembles a cesspit,
there will be no possibility for you to progress.

In short, YOUR LIFE IS AN ARTWORK.

You may proceed at your own pace, you may choose your own colours, you may choose what to portray, and you may choose whether or not it may benefit the spectator. Know that spectators there always are, even if you live apart as a hermit in a distant realm. Your task is to manifest the DIVINE in your artwork, in whatever fashion you choose, and thus can it serve as an inspiration to others who are not so far along the path.

We would like to invite you to consider very seriously everything we have said in this message, for the period of "examination" is upon you, and you will be presenting your "painting" shortly for inspection. You may think that we are speaking in riddles here, yet with time you will understand the meaning as well as the deep import of what we have been trying to convey to you. Seraphin

Seraphin Message 571
ON SEEING AS FAR AS ONE CAN SEE

Through Rosie, 28th August 2024

Dear Inhabitants on Earth; at this point in time – and we can reassure you that this is indeed a momentous junction in the history of your planet, when so much is 'on the move' – it will become increasingly clear to you that some people are entering an 'impasse', that is to say a dead end, yet they travel happily along this road, not looking left or right, but on the ground, blissfully unaware of the brick wall that they will be propelling into at full speed.

Please believe us when we say that there is absolutely nothing that you can do to prevent this. They have been already given many chances to turn in a different direction, and it has been their choice to ignore these chances. Thus, it is not your task at this late stage to make elaborate attempts to deter them, for you will not succeed.

On the contrary; if you attempt to do so, you will merely expend your own energy uselessly, and this energy could be so productively used to uplift others in some meritorious way.

What you can actually look out for is one of those persons who looks up for more than one second, who are genuinely in distress because they suspect – in the innermost part of themselves – that a bell is tolling for them, even if they do not recognise the import or the meaning.

If you discover such cases, and if you engage with such persons, you may have a chance of bringing them into the 'light'. We remind you that you are part of the divine cohorts of which there are many – which will bring the whole planet into 'life and light'. And despite all irritations and distractions, you can be sure that the bell tolls for EVERYONE.

The bells remind all that it is time to make an abiding moral choice, repudiating everything which is abusive, violent, discriminating, debilitating and destructive (especially the destruction of the DIVINE ELEMENT IN EVERYTHING).

The bell will remind you that there is not only one building - a church perhaps - from whence the sound comes, but that the whole world consists of a sacred 'church' and that each grain of sand and each living being is holy and called to live together in balance, harmony and love.

This wave of sound will be heard simultaneously by all,
but it will not have the same effect on all.

With some, it will uplift, and with some,
it will be too much to bear, and they will stumble to the ground.

Just as one can only see as far as one can see,
one can only hear as much as one is capable of hearing.

This may be old news to some of you,
yet despite your experience of time
as a divider between experiences to allow insight
and periods of learning and reflection,
this news is still very relevant to your NOW.

Sound is related to vibration, and everything on your earth
is inevitably destined to vibrate at a higher rate.

This is the choice your Earth has made
as part of her own spiritual journey.

We remind you of this greater scenario
because we see you becoming resigned.
We see you losing hope and turning to lesser things.

We ask you to look further than you can see,
IN THE SECURE KNOWLEDGE THAT THERE IS
A FORMIDABLE YET EXCITING NEW HORIZON AHEAD
WHICH WILL CHANGE YOUR VIEWPOINT
AND YOUR LIVES FOR THE BETTER.

Remember, the bells are tolling.

Seraphin.

Seraphin Message 572

CAREERING TOWARDS CHANGE
ON A STEEP DOWNWARD SLOPE

Through Rosie, 17th September 2024

If you are familiar with all the numerous Seraphin Messages, dear Inhabitants of Earth, you will notice that we have used various methods and various approaches and various tones to try and convey to you the diverse aspects of the problems you are facing, and which indeed mankind has created.

Our tone today is necessarily extremely strict, for as we have been warning again and again, the situation is escalating and is arriving at its most acute "peak". And from then on, it is a roller-coaster feeling of plummeting to depths you never knew existed, at a speed you have never before experienced, involving emotional turmoil of a sort you thought you would never go through.

Yet here it is: you are on that brink, and you will indeed be careering towards change at an incredible rate, and the downward slope is the steepest you can imagine.

As with all objects in velocity, it will be very difficult to avoid this course. Previously, when the pace was not so fast, it was possible to continue in a "roundabout way", taking deviations, taking time to investigate, entertain yourselves, distract yourselves, taking "holidays" or breaks as you thought fit.

But now all that has "disappeared down the rabbit hole". It will feel like everything is overtaking you, as if there is no time to breathe. Yet breathing will continue throughout, and if it all gets too much, it is this which we invite you to focus on to calm yourselves down - your breathing – which is a comforting constant and capable of steadying your nerves.

Be ready to "move" at any moment, whether this means in actual fact, fleeing a dangerous situation, or whether it means "moving" away from your beloved convictions and concepts.

Everything is destined to break,
apart from that which is DIVINE.
And in the end, only the DIVINE will remain.

What do we mean by this?

You are about to see the destruction of everything which does not fit into the DIVINE CATEGORY. Everything will be judged by that particular yardstick. We would say that this is the yardstick for the entire universe.

You may ask why this has not been applied to earth sooner (and you can be sure that the energies forcing the application of this yardstick do come from off-planet sources).

This can be explained by the fact that your planet has been granted DIVINE GRACE, which means that the normal necessary adhesion to cosmic law has been waivered for a designated period SO THAT YOU MAY COME TO VOLUNTARILY CHOOSE IT ALL BY YOURSELVES.

You have had the "free will" to choose this, to choose a moral path, to choose a path which benefits all humanity, to denounce corruption and abuse, yet this opportunity has not been chosen by the majority.

On the contrary, this lack of cosmic administration has been utilized and exploited by those who wish to exert power.

Such people think they are beyond the hand of cosmic authority, as has indeed been the case during this period of grace, YET THE EXPERIMENT IS NOW COMING TO AN END, and everyone will be called upon to assess and recognize their actions.

Those who do not recognize and regret their deviations will reap the consequences, for this your planet is again coming under cosmic law after a very long respite.

In this sense, there is an awful lot of work to be done, not only on a physical level, removing all that which is "not of god", but also on a mental level, for it is your thoughts and ideas which create the physical settings. It will be up to you to develop the exquisite sensitivity to your fellow human beings which will ensure that you all prosper and feel that you are in a place of great comfort and security.

The great majority of your lives at present is spent in fear, protecting your properties, belongings, livelihoods and in fact
EVERYTHING ELSE
against possible theft, demise, attack or abuse.

Imagine a world where all this no longer exists.
You will be part of the team which ensures this,
down to the very last details.
Eradication will be the first step.
Creating a better way will be the next step.

As you can imagine, the concept of "letting go" will be of extreme importance. Imagine, if you will that you have three minutes to leave the house before fire strikes. You can imagine how this concentrates the mind. You are forced to select what is most precious. Following such experiences, it will be clear that relationships are the most meaningful, that altruism is the most helpful, that solidarity with others is the most binding element that one could wish for.

You are about to enter an extreme situation of this nature, so we urge you to keep your wits about you at all times and be in frequent contact with your loved ones. Even if they momentarily reject such "alarmist announcements", you will be able to build a bridge to them later.

We look upon you all with some trepidation because we know that there are so many who are unprepared, and who will not know what has hit them.

Be loving towards them, for they know not what they do.

They will be helpless.
Remember that you also were once helpless,
and treat them accordingly.

We are surveying you during this final period of chaos.

Seraphin

THE COMPLETE SERAPHIN MESSAGES in 7 volumes

https://www.amazon.com/-/de/dp/B0CFLZGP6T

3 posters WISDOM FROM SERAPHIN:

POSTER A: https://www.artflakes.com/en/products/poster-a-wisdom-from-seraphin

POSTER B: https://www.artflakes.com/en/products/poster-b-wisdom-from-seraphin

POSTER C: https://www.artflakes.com/en/products/poster-c-wisdom-from-seraphin

ABOUT THE AUTHOR

ART - MUSIC - SERAPHIN MESSAGES - SEMINARS

Rosie Jackson is an author, artist, composer and the founder of *The Spiritual Revolution Project*. This encompasses paintings, music, videos, books and seminars to develop self-awareness. Teaching spiritual principles to promote consciousness, her music and art are intended as catalysts of spiritual uplift. Her *Unity Tarot* illustrates the transformation of 100 global villagers in 2 large paintings and 100 written biographies.

Since 2010, Rosie Jackson has been receiving telepathic messages and visions from the angel, Seraphin. These communications urge us to protect our earth and show us how paradise on earth can be achieved. Many messages are available in English, German, Italian, Spanish, Dutch and Korean.

Born in England, Rosie Jackson studied German and French and qualified as a teacher. She has worked as an instructor in China, and as a translator, designer and editor for publishing houses and companies in Europe. She is an artist, author and spiritual teacher in France, Germany and Italy.

rosie@rosiejackson.de.

ROSIE JACKSON'S WEBSITES

ART PRINTS:
https://www.artflakes.com/en/s?search=Rosie+Jackson

MAIN WEBSITE:
www.rosiejackson.de

MUSIC ALBUM:
https://rjspirit100.bandcamp.com/album/songs-for-the-era-of-light-and-life

SEMINARS:
http://www.rosie-jackson.de/revolution/Seminar_Termine.html

INSTAGRAM:
https://www.instagram.com/rjspirit100/

THE SPIRITUAL REVOLUTION PROJECT:
http://www.rosie-jackson.de/revolution/Projekt_und_Vision.html

MUSIC/ART VIDEOS:
https://www.youtube.com/cha-nel/UCMCeJnqJ9Y7hqAExYmm9iKA

OTHER PUBLICATIONS BY ROSIE JACKSON

The Unity Tarot
ISBN 978-3-754342565

Seraphin's Spirituality School: ISBN 978-3-749485-84-0

The Complete Seraphin Messages: Volume 1
ISBN 978-3-751976-72-5 (Seraphin Series: Book 4)

The Complete Seraphin Messages: Volume 2
ISBN 978-3-75198150-7 (Seraphin Series: Book 5)

The Complete Seraphin Messages: Volume 3
ISBN 978-3-75190001-0 (Seraphin Series: Book 6)

The Complete Seraphin Messages: Volume 4
ISBN 978-3-752 643275 (Seraphin Series: Book 7)

The Complete Seraphin Messages: Volume 5
ISBN 978-3-753444741 (Seraphin Series: Book 8)

The Complete Seraphin Messages: Volume 6
ISBN 978-3-754356951 (Seraphin Series: Book 9)

The Complete Seraphin Messages: Volume 7
ISBN 978-3-757846824 (Seraphin Series: Book 10)

The World will become Peaceful, Beautiful and Abundant
ISBN 978-3-751920-66-7 (Seraphin Series: Book 2)

The Peace Parables: ISBN 978-3-750441-51-4

The Absolutely Amazing Activity Book: ISBN 978-3-8370-0238-6

**Wie das Schweinchen Prinzessin Prunella
das Lachen lernte**: ISBN 978-3-749428-85-4

**Ich bin Lebendigkeit: Eine Reise zu mehr Authentizität,
Kraft und Freude**: ISBN 978-3937883-32-8

Rosie Jackson

AN ANGEL SPEAKS
SERAPHIN'S SPIRITUALITY SCHOOL
YOUR DIVINE ROLE:
CREATING AN ERA OF PEACE

ISBN 978-3-749485-84-0. 2019. 292 pages

Seraphin is an angel who send us messages of hope and inspiration, as well as practical advice. Our world requires a drastic makeover, and this will be fueled by a universal change of heart, by widening our perspectives, and by reconnecting to the divine core within us, which impels us to develop our skills in service to humanity.

Seraphin's statements provide remarkable insights, provoke intense reflection, and challenge our limited viewpoint. With great clarity, he points out the necessity for radical change, while knowing that we have the power to implement it. The messages in this book were received telepathically by Rosie Jackson.

This collection of 111 Seraphin Messages has 5 purposes. The first chapter, "Messages from the other side" encouraging readers to start a writing journey, contacting their unseen guides and "downloading" information relevant to their particular task on earth. As your spiritual abilities progress, you will increase in confidence, and you will become a source of inspiration for others.

Secondly, the chapters entitled "Your divine purpose", "Transcending your past", "Creating your future", and "Your relationships", intend to help readers along the spiritual path, assisting them to develop potential, achieve excellency, and use these skills and knowledge for the benefit of all.

Chapter 3, "Preparing for transition", provides advice on how to deal with the intense times ahead. Due to our present position in the photon belt, our planet is showered with highly powered cosmic energies.

These create enormous change, supporting everything of divine nature, and exposing that which is not.

Fourthly, the chapters on rebuilding our world offer instructions on how to address practical problems. They also highlight which qualities we should manifest in order to maintain peace, beauty and abundance on our world.

Fifthly, the goal of the very last chapter, "Reconnecting to the universe", aims to increase our awareness of our galactic neighbours who lovingly observe us. After millennia of "disconnection", we will finally resume our membership of the cosmic family.

Rosie Jackson

THE ABSOLUTELY AMAZING ACTIVITY BOOK OF
SNAKES, STARS AND SNOWBALLS
FURTHERING CREATIVE EXPRESSION
IN CHILDREN FROM THE AGE OF 7 UP

ISBN: 978-3-8370-0238-6. 80 pages

Each of these 80 pages presents a story, idea, or situation which stimulates children's imagination through questions, suggestions or invitations to wonder what happens next. The pictures they then draw are subconscious images of their inner world, feelings and desires, thus providing their carers with a valuable window to their soul.

Once children are accustomed to expressing their own emotions and needs, they are better able to assess themselves and others on the path towards mutual understanding and peace. Like SNAKES they can shed their old skins, like SNOWBALLS they can move on and grow, reaching more and more towards the stars.

Rosie Jackson

THE UNITY TAROT

CHOOSE A NUMBER BETWEEN 1 AND 100 TO FIND SOLUTIONS

ISBN 978-3-754342565. 241 pages.

100 stories of transformation from around the world

100 qualities which promote harmony and peace

1000 questions which point us in a new, better direction

The Unity Tarot offers a new and novel way of addressing problematic issues. Intuitively choose a number between 1 and 100 and see which positive quality you are invited to increase to solve your dilemma.

The accompanying stories are designed to assist readers on their spiritual journey, opening up new vistas, opportunities and directions. They provide insights, shake up superstitions, encourage action and creativity, dissipate stagnation, break our slave mentality, revive creative powers, invite reassessment and foster true values.

The Unity Tarot has breathtaking potential to implement changes in our outlook, beliefs, behavior and abilities, taking us to the higher level of consciousness which is so necessary for the peace and prosperity of our planet.

THE WORLD WILL BECOME
PEACEFUL, BEAUTIFUL AND ABUNDANT

A compact instruction manual:
150 ways to improve our world

ISBN 9783751920667.196 pages

Our desecrated, ravaged earth requires massive overhaul.

WHAT CAN WE DO? This instruction book for individuals and groups presents 150 methods of making the world peaceful, beautiful and abundant. They focus on personal, social, cultural, environmental and global RESPONSIBILITIES. Most important, however, is the recognition of our divine responsibilities:

"We are the drop of water in a polluted ocean. We are a genetically manipulated seed planted in a field which has been doused with artificial fertiliser. We are a small tender plant strangled by rampant weeds. We are a million stars in a far-flung galaxy.

If we can take on these roles, we will ask WHY and search for solutions. If we are in polluted water, we will seek METHODS OF PURIFICATION. If we are a genetically manipulated seed, we will seek METHODS TO REVERSE ADVERSE PROGRAMING. If we are planted in contaminated soil, we will seek METHODS TO REGENERATE NATURALLY. If we are strangled by weeds, we will seek METHODS OF CLEARING THE MENTAL JUNGLE. And if we are a million stars, we will be encouraged to LIVE OUR INFINITE POTENTIAL AND SPREAD LIGHT ETERNALLY".

These poetic as well as practical pearls of wisdom have been provided by the angel Seraphin, and have been received telepathically between 2009 and 2020 by the author and artist, Rosie Jackson.

Rosie Jackson

THE PEACE PARABLES:
HOW THE FOOL BECAME GOD,
AND OTHER STORIES

ISBN 9783750441514, 140 pages

What do the stories with the titles INSIDE THE MARBLE and THE ROOF and THE EMERGENCY BRAKE have in common? Like the other 53 stories in this volume, they are "peace parables" because they urge us to improve our behaviour, not only for our own benefit, but for the common good, enabling us to co-create a peaceful world. Most of these parables are descriptions of visions received during meditation by the author and artist, Rosie Jackson. Some are adaptations of messages received telepathically from the angel, Seraphin.

One of the most famous storytellers is the soul we call Jesus. Parables are an excellent way of teaching, as they entertain and educate people of various paths simultaneously, without raising an accusing finger. No one is addressed personally. It is up to readers to draw their own conclusions. All these parables are designed to assist readers on their spiritual journey, opening up new vistas, opportunities and directions. The stories provide insights, shake up superstitions, encourage heroic acts, expose corruption, pinpoint our enslaved mentalities, reveal our debilitating dependence, revive our dormant creative powers, invite reassessment of the "status quo", reveal downward spirals, discourage materialism, inspire love of nature and foster true values.

The stories entertain and educate, urging us to search for better solutions, to increase compassion and recognise our interconnection. They illuminate dangerous domino effects, and expose our narrow-mindedness and blind allegiance. These stories prepare us to be flexible in the face of great change, and force us to reflect upon our LIFE'S PURPOSE.

THE SPIRITUAL REVOLUTION PROJECT

In 2005, the artist Rosie Jackson made a mental note of the fact that different people were always sending her the same text which began "If the world was a village of 100 people", and she decided that this was not coincidence, but divine synchronicity. Using the global statistics in this text (concerning nationality, religion, living conditions etc.) she invented 100 "global villagers" – each of whom represented 1% of the global population - and wrote their biographies. Then she depicted these "global villagers" in a 5-metre-long painting entitled THE WORLD-REALITY, illustrating the whole range of human problems on earth.

But having done this, she felt she could not just leave it at that, so she spent another 2 years considering how each of the 100 global villagers could turn their lives around if they pursued a certain "positive" quality (such as respect, gratitude or compassion). Then she painted the 100 figures anew, depicting their transformation, in another large painting entitled THE WORLD-VISION. The 100 positive qualities act as the catalyst for the SPIRITUAL REVOLUTION which can transform our world into paradise. The 100 biographies all have a "happy end" and include 10 pertinent questions, and this now forms the UNITY TAROT which is used as the basis for Rosie's seminars.

100 TRANSFORMATIVE QUALITIES IN THE UNITY TAROT

What qualities must we develop to ensure peace and become "one"? The UNITY TAROT offers 100 "positive" qualities which can serve as a point of orientation. The more we voluntarily and conscientiously adhere to them out of love for ourselves and our fellow humans, the faster we will move towards harmonious living. The transformation of the 100 global villagers does not lie in increased material wealth but in increased demonstration of these positive qualities.

SPIRITUAL REVOLUTION SEMINARS

In the course of these seminars, participants encounter everything which separates them from others (culture, customs, beliefs). At the same time, they discover mutual ground, which is the world of feelings and emotions, how we conduct our relationships, how we deal with our fears and problems, and how we express our sadness and joy.

Simultaneously, participants celebrate their miraculous diversity and potential. As troubadours of a new peaceful age, it is their intent to spread the wisdom, insights and loving attitude acquired during this process. If participants SPECIFICALLY INTEND to represent 1% of the global population, then their personal work on themselves will also positively affect this 1%, working through the morphogenetic field.

The vision of the Spiritual Revolution Project is that these seminars and processes take place worldwide and that participants from many countries built up partnerships with each other. Participants are also invited to search for their chosen "global villager" in real life, and to record their experience in articles / film / photographs as part of the project 100 SEEK 100.

PROJECT: ARTISTS CREATE PEACE

"The arts are not simply for amusement, distraction, representation or financial investment. They are a form of worship or service capable of awakening spiritual faculties and perspectives. We pledge to further the ARTS as A SACRED ACT WHERE EVERY BRUSHSTROKE AND TUNE AND MOVEMENT CAN BE CONDUCTED AS A PRAYER WHICH BLESSES AND ACCELERATES OUR JOURNEY TOWARDS PARADISE"

(From *The Artists' Manifesto*, Rosie Jackson)

FOR YOUR NOTES: